KITCHEN TABLE

100 Cakes and Bakes

KITCHEN TABLE gives you a wealth of recipes from your favourite chefs. Whether you want a quick weekday supper, sumptuous weekend feast or food for friends and family, let Rick, Ken, Madhur, Antonio, Ainsley, Mary and Annabel bring their expertise to your table.

For exclusive recipes, our regular newsletter, blog and news about Apps for your phone, visit www.mykitchentable.co.uk

Throughout this book, when you see visit our site for practical videos, tips and hints from the My Kitchen Table team.

KITCHEN
TABLE

100 Cakes and Bakes
MARY BERRY

www.mykitchentable.co.uk

Welcome to (my) KITCHEN TABLE

I have turned to the **100 cake and bake recipes** collected here many times over the years for inspiration when baking for my family – I hope you enjoy trying them too.

Mary Berry

Contents

Victoria Sandwich

A great British classic. The all-in-one method makes it very simple to prepare. Vary the jam as you wish.

Step one Preheat the oven to 180°C/Fan 160°C/gas 4. Lightly grease the sandwich tins and then line the bases with non-stick baking parchment.

Step two Measure the butter, sugar, eggs, flour and the baking powder into a large bowl and beat for about 2 minutes, until just blended; an electric mixer is best for this, but of course you can also beat by hand with a wooden spoon.

Step three Divide the mixture between the prepared tins and level the surface with the back of a spoon or a plastic spatula.

Step four Bake for about 25 minutes, until well risen and golden. The tops of the cakes should spring back when pressed lightly with a finger. Leave the cakes to cool in the tins for a few minutes, then run a small palette knife or blunt knife around the edge of the tins to free the sides of the cakes. Turn the cakes out onto a wire rack, peel off the paper and leave to cool completely.

Step five Choose the cake with the best top, then put the other cake top down onto a serving plate. Spread with the jam, put the other cake on top (top uppermost) and sprinkle with caster sugar to serve.

Cake tins needed:
2 loose-based 20cm
(8in) sandwich tins
4cm (1½ in) deep

225g (8oz) butter,
softened

225g (8oz) caster
sugar

4 large eggs

225g (8oz) self-raising
flour

2 level tsp baking
powder

**for the filling and
topping**

about 4 tbsp
strawberry or
raspberry jam

a little caster sugar

For step-by-step photographs of this recipe, go to
www.mykitchentable.co.uk/recipes/victoriasandwich

Swiss Roll

This fat-free sponge is a good alternative to a round cake at teatime.
The filling can be easily jazzed up to serve the Swiss roll as a dessert.

Cake tin needed:
a 33 x 23cm (13 x 9in)
Swiss roll tin

4 large eggs

100g (4oz) caster
sugar

100g (4oz) self-raising
flour

for the filling

4 tbsp strawberry or
raspberry jam

Step one Preheat the oven to 220°C/Fan 200°C/gas 7. Grease the tin and line with non-stick baking parchment. Whisk the eggs and sugar together in a large bowl until the mixture is light and frothy and the whisk leaves a trail when lifted out.

Step two Sift the flour into the mixture, carefully folding it in. Turn the mixture into the tin and give it a gentle shake so that the mixture finds its own level, making sure that it spreads evenly into the corners. Bake for about 10 minutes or until the sponge is golden brown and begins to shrink from the edges of the tin.

Step three While the cake is cooking, place a piece of non-stick baking parchment a little bigger than the size of the tin onto a work surface and sprinkle it with caster sugar.

Step four Once the cake is cooked, invert it onto the sugared parchment. Quickly loosen the parchment on the bottom of the cake and peel it off. Trim the edges of the sponge with a sharp knife and make a score mark 2.5cm (1in) in from one shorter edge, being careful not to cut right through.

Step five Leave to cool slightly, then spread with the jam. If the cake is too hot the jam will soak straight into the sponge. Roll up the cake firmly from the cut end.

To make a smaller Swiss Roll, use 3 large eggs and 75g (3oz) each of sugar and flour. Bake in a greased and lined 28 x 18cm (11 x 7in) Swiss roll tin.

To make a Coffee Swiss Roll, fill the basic Swiss Roll with coffee butter cream made with 75g (3oz) softened butter, 225g (8oz) sifted icing sugar, 2 teaspoons of milk and 2 teaspoons of coffee essence.

To make a Chocolate Swiss Roll, instead of 100g (4oz) self-raising flour, use 65g (2⅛oz) self-raising flour and 40g (1½oz) cocoa powder, and fill the cooked roll with whipped cream.

Black Cherry Swiss Roll

This classic teatime cake is best eaten very fresh, as fat-free sponges do not keep for long. Vary the jam as you wish.

Step one Preheat the oven to 200°C/Fan 180°C/gas 6. Cut a rectangle of non-stick baking parchment just larger than the base and sides of the Swiss roll tin. Grease the tin and then line it with the paper, pushing it neatly into the corners to fit.

Step two Put the eggs and sugar in a large bowl and whisk well, until the mixture is light and frothy and the whisk leaves a trail when lifted out

Step three Sift the flour into the mixture, carefully folding it in at the same time with a plastic spatula. Turn the mixture into the prepared tin and spread it gently into the corners. Bake for 10 minutes or until the sponge begins to shrink away from the sides of the tin and is springy to the touch. Watch the cake very carefully as it is easy to overbake it.

Step four While the cake is cooking, place a piece of non-stick baking parchment a little bigger than the size of the tin on a work surface and sprinkle it with caster sugar.

Step five When the cake is cooked, invert it onto the sugared paper. Quickly loosen the lining paper on the bottom of the cake and peel it away. Trim the edges of the sponge with a sharp knife and make a score mark 2.5cm (1in) in from one shorter edge, being careful not to cut right through.

Step six Roll the cake up firmly from the shorter, cut end, with the paper inside, and leave to cool. Carefully unroll the cooled cake, remove the paper and spread the cake with the jam, followed by the whipped cream. Re-roll the cake, sprinkle with a little more caster sugar if you like, and, for a special occasion, decorate with a few fresh black cherries. Keep in the fridge until needed but eat as fresh as possible.

Cake tin needed:
a 33 x 23cm (13 x 9in) Swiss roll tin

4 large eggs, at room temperature

100g (4oz) caster sugar, plus extra for sprinkling

100g (4oz) self-raising flour

for the filling

about 3 tbsp black cherry jam

300ml (½ pint) pouring double cream, whipped

a few fresh black cherries (optional)

The Ultimate Chocolate Roulade

Always popular, this roulade freezes very well. Raspberries and chocolate are good together, so add some raspberries (frozen are fine) to the filling if you wish. For a special occasion, scatter masses of fresh raspberries around the roulade on the serving platter – it looks stunning.

Cake tin needed:
a 33 x 23cm (13 x 9in) Swiss roll tin

175g (6oz) plain chocolate (39 per cent cocoa solids), broken into pieces

175g (6oz) caster sugar

6 large eggs, separated

2 tbsp cocoa powder, sifted

300ml (½ pint) pouring double cream

icing sugar

Step one Preheat the oven to 180°C/Fan 160°C/gas 4. Lightly grease the Swiss roll tin and line with non-stick baking parchment, pushing it into the corners.

Step two Put the chocolate into a bowl placed over a pan of hot water. The water in the pan must not touch the bowl or the chocolate may overheat. Place the pan over a low heat until the chocolate has melted, stirring occasionally. Allow to cool slightly.

Step three Put the sugar and egg yolks into a bowl and whisk with a hand-held electric mixer on a high speed until light and creamy. Add the cooled chocolate and stir until evenly blended. Whisk the egg whites in a large mixing bowl until stiff but not dry. Stir a large spoonful of the egg whites into the chocolate mixture, mix gently and then fold in the remaining egg whites followed by the cocoa powder.

Step four Turn the mixture into the prepared tin and gently level the surface. Bake for about 20 minutes, until firm to the touch. Remove the cake from the oven, leave in the tin and place a cooling rack over the top of the cake. Place a clean, damp tea towel on top of the rack and leave for several hours or overnight in a cool place; the cake will sink slightly. (If the tea towel dries out, simply re-dampen it.)

Step five Whip the cream until it just holds its shape. Dust a large piece of non-stick baking parchment with icing sugar. Turn the roulade out onto the paper and peel off the lining paper. Spread with the whipped cream and roll up like a Swiss roll, starting with one of the short edges; roll tightly to start with and use the paper to help. Don't worry if it cracks – that is quite normal and part of its charm!

Battenburg Cake

You can use either home-made or bought almond paste, or marzipan, for this famous chequerboard cake.

Step one Preheat the oven to 160°C/Fan 140°C/gas 3. Grease the tin and line the base with non-stick baking parchment.

Step two Measure the butter, sugar, eggs, ground rice, flour, baking powder and almond extract into a large bowl and beat for about 2 minutes until smooth. Spoon half the mixture into the right half of the prepared tin as neatly as possible. Add a few drops of red food colouring to the remaining mixture to turn it a deep pink colour, then spoon this into the left half of the tin. Try to make the join between the 2 mixtures as neat as possible. Smooth the surface of each half.

Step three Bake for 35–40 minutes or until the cake is well risen, springy to the touch and has shrunk slightly from the sides of the tin. Leave to cool in the tin for a few minutes then turn out, peel off the parchment and finish cooling on a wire rack. Trim the edges of the cake when cool and then cut into four equal strips – you need two pink and two plain strips of equal size.

Step four Gently heat the apricot jam in a small pan. Use the warmed jam to stick the four strips of cake together to make a chequerboard effect. Brush the top of the assembled cake with apricot jam.

Step five Roll out the almond paste or marzipan into an oblong the length of the cake and sufficiently wide to wrap around the cake. Invert the cake onto the almond paste or marzipan, then brush the remaining 3 sides with apricot jam. Press the almond paste or marzipan neatly around the cake, arranging the join in one corner. Score the top of the cake with a criss cross pattern to decorate.

Cake tin needed:
a shallow 18cm (7in)
square cake tin

100g (4oz) butter,
softened

100g (4oz) caster
sugar

2 large eggs

50g (2oz) ground rice

100g (4oz) self-raising
flour

½ level tsp baking
powder

a few drops almond
extract

red food colouring

to finish

3–4 tbsp apricot jam

225g (8oz) almond
paste or marzipan

Carrot Cake with Mascarpone Topping

Always a popular cake, this American carrot cake needs to be stored in the fridge because of the mascarpone topping. Walnut pieces are cheaper than walnut halves and are perfect for using in cakes.

Cake tin needed:
a deep, round 20cm (8in) cake tin

225g (8oz) self-raising flour

2 level tsp baking powder

150g (5oz) light muscovado sugar

50g (2oz) walnut pieces, chopped

100g (4oz) carrots, coarsely grated

2 ripe bananas, mashed

2 large eggs

150ml (¼ pint) sunflower oil

for the topping

250g (9oz) mascarpone cheese

2–3 tsp vanilla extract

2 tbsp icing sugar, sifted

about 25g (1oz) walnut pieces, chopped

Step one Preheat the oven to 180°C/Fan 160°C/gas 4. Lightly grease the cake tin and line the base with non-stick baking parchment.

Step two Put all the ingredients for the cake into a large bowl and mix until thoroughly blended; an electric mixer is best for this, but of course you can also beat by hand with a wooden spoon. Turn the mixture into the prepared tin and gently level the surface.

Step three Bake for 50–60 minutes, until the cake is well risen, golden and beginning to shrink away from the sides of the tin. A fine skewer inserted into the centre of the cake should come out clean. Allow the cake to cool in the tin for a few minutes, then loosen the side of the cake from the tin with a small palette knife or a blunt knife, turn the cake out onto a wire rack and leave to cool completely.

Step four For the topping, put the mascarpone cheese into a small bowl, add the vanilla extract, icing sugar and walnuts and beat together. Spread evenly over the top of the cake. Store the iced cake in the fridge.

KITCHEN TABLE

For Mary Berry's tips on how to line a baking tin, go to www.mykitchentable.co.uk/author/MaryBerry/tips

Maple Syrup Cake

Using maple syrup and pecan nuts, this Canadian-inspired cake is filled and covered with whipped cream, and is a real treat for a special gathering at coffee time. Fill and cover ahead of time, so that the cake keeps moist. Only the orange zest is used, so add the flesh from the oranges to a fruit salad or have fresh orange for breakfast.

Step one Preheat the oven to 160°C/Fan 140°C/gas 3. Lightly grease the cake tin and then line the base with non-stick baking parchment.

Step two Put all the ingredients for the cake except the pecan nuts into a large bowl and mix well until evenly blended. Stir in the chopped pecan nuts.

Step three Spoon the mixture into the cake tin and level the surface. Bake for 1–1½ hours, until well risen, golden and springy to the touch. Allow to cool slightly, then turn the cake out onto a wire rack, peel off the lining paper and leave to cool completely.

Step four Whip the cream until it just holds its shape and then fold in the maple syrup.

Step five Split the cake horizontally into three and fill and cover with the cream, using a small palette knife to smooth it evenly over the top and sides. Decorate the top with the orange zest. Store in the refrigerator.

Cake tin needed: a deep, round 20cm (8in) cake tin

225g (8oz) butter, softened

225g (8oz) light muscovado sugar

zest of 1 orange

4 large eggs

100ml (3½ fl oz) maple syrup

350g (12oz) self-raising flour

2 level tsp baking powder

¼ level tsp ground ginger

50g (2oz) pecan nuts, chopped

for the filling and topping

460ml (15fl oz) pouring double cream

2 tbsp maple syrup

zest of 1 orange

For a video masterclass on icing a cake, go to www.mykitchentable.co.uk/videos/icing

Cappuccino Cake

Make sure you use deep sandwich tins for this recipe, as the shallower tins tend to overflow. They are available from good cookshops or by mail order.

Cake tins needed:
2 loose-based 20cm (8in) sandwich tins, 4cm (1½ in) deep

50g (2oz) cocoa powder

6 tbsp boiling water

3 large eggs

60ml (2fl oz) milk

175g (6oz) self-raising flour

1 rounded tsp baking powder

100g (4oz) butter, softened

275g (10oz) caster sugar

for the filling and topping

300ml (½ pint) pouring double cream

1 level tsp instant coffee, dissolved in 2 tsp hot water

a little cocoa powder or drinking chocolate, for dusting

Step one Preheat the oven to 180°C/Fan 160°C/gas 4. Lightly grease both the tins and line the bases with non-stick baking parchment.

Step two Put the cocoa powder into a large mixing bowl, add the boiling water and mix well until it has a paste-like consistency.

Step three Add all the remaining ingredients to the bowl and whisk with a hand-held electric mixer until just combined. The mixture will be a thickish batter (be careful not to overwhisk).

Step four Divide the cake mixture between the prepared tins and gently level the surface. Bake for 25–30 minutes, until the cakes are well risen and beginning to shrink away from the side of the tin. Turn the cakes out onto a wire rack and leave to cool completely.

Step five To finish the cake, whip the double cream until it just holds its shape and then stir in the dissolved coffee. Use half the cream to fill the cake and spread the remainder over the top. Gently smooth the surface with a palette knife and dust with sifted cocoa or drinking chocolate. This cake is best eaten fresh; store in the fridge if necessary.

For Mary Berry's guide to baking equipment, go to
www.mykitchentable.co.uk/authors/MaryBerry/equipment

Frosted Walnut Layer Cake

This is a truly old-fashioned cake iced with a simple 'American frosting' of sweet whipped egg white.

Step one Preheat the oven to 160°C/Fan 140°C/gas 3. Grease the tins then line the base of each tin with non-stick baking parchment.

Step two Measure all the ingredients for the cake into a large bowl and beat until thoroughly blended. Divide the mixture equally between the tins and level the surfaces.

Step three Bake for 25–30 minutes until the cakes are golden and springy to the touch. Leave to cool in the tin for a few minutes then turn out, peel off the parchment and finish cooling on a wire rack.

Step four To make the frosting, measure all the ingredients into a bowl over a pan of hot water and whisk for 10–12 minutes until thick. Sandwich the cake layers together with a little of the frosting, then use the remainder to cover the top and sides of the cake, swirling the icing to form softened peaks. Work quickly as the icing sets rapidly. Leave to set in a cool place, but not in the fridge.

Step five Decorate with the walnut halves.

Don't be tempted to use more baking powder than specified, or the cake will rise up and then sink back again. In this all-in-one method, self-raising flour and baking powder are used together to give the cake the necessary lift. The quickness of the method means that less air is whisked into the mixture than if the cake is made the traditional way.

Cake tins needed:
3 x 20cm (8in) sandwich tins

225g (8oz) butter, softened

225g (8oz) caster sugar

4 large eggs

225g (8oz) self-raising flour

2 level tsp baking powder

100g (4oz) walnuts, finely chopped

for the frosting

2 large egg whites

350g (12oz) caster sugar

4 tbsp water

¼ level tsp cream of tartar

to decorate

walnut halves

Very Best Chocolate Fudge Cake

This will become your favourite chocolate cake recipe – it is the best! It is speedy to make and the easy filling doubles as an icing. The cake is moist and has a 'grown-up' chocolate flavour.

Cake tins needed:
2 deep 20cm (8in) sandwich tins

50g (2oz) sifted cocoa powder

6 tbsp boiling water

3 large eggs

50ml (2fl oz) milk

175g (6oz) self-raising flour

1 rounded tsp baking powder

100g (4oz) butter, softened

275g (10oz) caster sugar

for the icing and filling

3 tbsp apricot jam

150g (5oz) plain chocolate (39 per cent cocoa solids)

150ml (¼ pint) pouring double cream

Step one Preheat the oven to 180°C/Fan 160°C/gas 4. Grease the tins, then line the base of each tin with non-stick baking parchment.

Step two Blend the cocoa and boiling water in a large bowl then add the remaining cake ingredients and beat until the mixture has become a smooth, thickish batter. Divide the mixture equally between the prepared tins and level the surface.

Step three Bake for 25–30 minutes or until well risen and the tops of the cakes spring back when lightly pressed with a finger. Leave to cool in the tins for a few minutes, then turn out, peel off the parchment and finish cooling on a wire rack.

Step four To make the icing, warm the apricot jam in a very small pan, then spread a little over the base of one cake and the top of the other. Break the chocolate into pieces and gently heat with the cream in a heatproof bowl set over a pan of simmering water for about 10 minutes or just until the chocolate has melted, stirring occasionally. Remove the bowl from the heat and stir the mixture to make sure the chocolate has completely melted. Leave to cool until it is on the point of setting then spread on top of the apricot on both cakes.

Step five Sandwich the cakes together and use a small palette knife to smooth the icing on the top. Keep in a cool place until ready to serve.

The cake can be frozen (iced or un-iced) for up to 1 month. Store in a round freezer-proof container about 2.5cm (1in) bigger than the diameter of the cake. Sit the cake on the inside of the lid and place the container over the top. Seal, label and freeze. If the cake is frozen iced, the icing will not be quite as shiny once thawed. To defrost, release the lid but leave in position and thaw for 4 hours at room temperature.

Death by Chocolate Cake

I have given a generous amount of icing to fill and ice this cake, as it should be sheer luxury and a complete indulgence! The icing is very easy to make, but take care not to overheat it or it will lose its shine. For the same reason, don't store the cake in the fridge – a cool place is fine.

Step one Preheat the oven to 160°C/Fan 140°C/gas 3. Grease both the tins and line the bases with non-stick baking parchment.

Step two Sift the flour, cocoa powder, bicarbonate of soda and baking powder into a large bowl. Add the sugar and mix well.

Step three Make a well in the centre of the dry ingredients and add the golden syrup, eggs, oil and milk. Beat well, using a wooden spoon, until smooth and then pour into the tins.

Step four Bake for about 35 minutes, until the cakes are well risen and spring back when pressed lightly with the fingertips. Turn out onto a wire rack, remove the lining paper and leave to cool completely. Cut each cake in half horizontally.

Step five To make the icing, put the chocolate into a bowl placed over a pan of hot water. The water in the pan must not touch the bowl or the chocolate may overheat. Place the pan over a low heat until the chocolate has melted, stirring occasionally, then add the butter and stir until the butter has melted.

Step six Put the bottom half of one cake on a wire rack and place a baking sheet underneath to catch the drips. Spoon a little of the icing onto the cake and spread it evenly to the sides. Repeat with the remaining cake layers, then pour the remaining icing over the top of the cake and smooth it evenly over the top and sides of the cake. Leave to set.

Step seven To make the chocolate waves, melt the chocolates in separate small bowls over a pan of hot water. Spread the chocolate onto four strips of foil about 4cm (1½in) wide and 35cm (14in) long. Lay the strips carefully over 2 tins, placed on their sides on a baking sheet, to give a wavy shape. Allow to set in the fridge, then carefully peel off the foil and use.

Cake tins needed:
2 loose-based 20cm (8in) sandwich tins, 4cm (1½in) deep

275g (10oz) plain flour

3 tbsp cocoa powder

1½ level tsp bicarbonate of soda

1½ level tsp baking powder

215g (7½oz) caster sugar

3 tbsp golden syrup

3 large eggs, beaten

225ml (8fl oz) sunflower oil

225ml (8fl oz) milk

for the icing

450g (1lb) plain chocolate (39 per cent cocoa solids), broken into pieces

200g (7oz) unsalted butter

for the chocolate waves

about 50g (2oz) each white and plain chocolate (39 per cent cocoa solids)

Farmhouse Orange Victoria Sandwich

A very special cake, and beautifully moist.

Cake tins needed:
2 x 18cm (7in)
sandwich cake tins

175g (6oz) butter,
softened

175g (6oz) light
muscovado sugar

3 large eggs

175g (6oz) self-raising
flour

1½ level tsp baking
powder

zest of 1 orange

for the filling

40g (1½ oz) butter,
softened

100g (4oz) icing sugar,
sieved

1–2 tbsp fine-cut
marmalade

icing sugar, sieved,
for dusting

Step one Preheat the oven to 180°C/Fan 160°C/gas 4. Grease the tins and line the bases with non-stick baking parchment.

Step two Measure all the ingredients for the cake into a bowl and beat well for about 2 minutes, until smooth and blended. Divide the mixture between the tins evenly and level out.

Step three Bake for 25-30 minutes or until the cakes have shrunk away slightly from the sides of the tins and will spring back when lightly pressed with a finger. Turn out the cakes onto a wire rack to cool and peel off the paper.

Step four Measure the ingredients for the filling into a bowl and blend together until smooth. Use to sandwich the cakes together. Dust the top of the cake with sieved icing sugar.

Hokey Pokey Coffee Cake

A special cake from New Zealand. Coffee and walnuts have a natural affinity and make a delicious cake. The addition of walnut praline makes this extra special.

Step one Preheat the oven to 160°C/Fan 140°C/gas 3. Lightly grease both the tins and line the bases with non-stick baking parchment.

Step two Measure all the ingredients for the cake into a mixing bowl and beat until thoroughly blended. Divide the mixture evenly between the prepared tins and gently level the surface with the back of a spoon or a plastic spatula.

Step three Bake for 30–35 minutes until the cakes are well risen, golden and beginning to shrink away from the sides of the tins. The tops of the cakes should spring back when lightly pressed with a finger. Allow the cakes to cool in the tins for a few minutes, then run a small palette knife or blunt knife around the edge of the cakes to loosen them. Turn out onto a wire rack, peel off the paper and leave to cool completely.

Step four While the cakes are baking, you can make the praline. Put the water and caster sugar into a small pan and heat gently until the sugar dissolves. Continue to cook slowly until the sugar turns to a nut brown. Watch the pan like a hawk, as the sugar can burn quickly. Off the heat, stir in the walnuts, then pour the mixture out onto non-stick baking parchment or an oiled baking sheet and leave to cool completely.

Step five Roughly break up the cold, hard praline with your fingers. Save the best pieces for the top of the cake, then chop the remainder to add to the icing for the middle of the cake.

Step six To make the icing, put the butter, icing sugar and coffee into a bowl and mix well until evenly blended. Select the cake with the best top, then place the other cake top down on a serving plate. Spread with half the icing and add the chopped praline. Place the second cake on top and spread with the remaining butter icing. Decorate with the reserved walnut praline pieces.

Cake tins needed:
2 loose-based 20cm (8in) sandwich tins 4cm (1½in) deep

225g (8oz) butter, softened

225g (8oz) caster sugar

4 large eggs

225g (8oz) self-raising flour

1 level tsp baking powder

1½ tbsp instant coffee, mixed with 1 tbsp hot water

75g (3oz) walnuts, chopped

for the walnut praline

2 tbsp water

50g (2oz) caster sugar

50g (2oz) walnut pieces

for the butter icing

75g (3oz) butter, softened

250g (9oz) icing sugar, sifted

1½ level tsp instant coffee, dissolved in 1½ tbsp hot water

Cherry Cake

This classic English cake is perfect to serve with tea. To prevent the cherries sinking to the bottom during cooking, wash the quartered cherries, then dry thoroughly on kitchen paper before adding them to the cake mixture.

Cake tin needed:
a deep, round 18cm (7in) cake tin

150g (5oz) glacé cherries

225g (8oz) self-raising flour

50g (2oz) ground almonds

1½ level tsp baking powder

200g (7oz) butter, softened

200g (7oz) caster sugar

4 large eggs

Step one Preheat the oven to 160°C/Fan 140°C/gas 3. Lightly grease the cake tin and line the base with non-stick baking parchment.

Step two Cut each cherry into quarters and rinse under cold running water to remove excess syrup. Drain well and dry thoroughly on kitchen paper.

Step three Measure all the remaining ingredients into a large bowl and beat well for about 1 minute to mix thoroughly. Carefully fold in the prepared cherries.

Step four Turn the mixture into the tin and bake for 1–1½ hours, until the cake is well risen, golden and firm to the touch. A fine skewer inserted into the centre of the cake should come out clean. Leave the cake to cool in the tin for about 10 minutes, then turn it out onto a wire rack and leave to cool completely.

Almond Spice Cake

A thin layer of sweet almond paste is baked through the centre of this cake, and works very well with the warming flavours of cinnamon and clove.

Step one Preheat the oven to 180°C/Fan 160°C/gas 4. Grease the tin, then line the base with non-stick baking parchment.

Step two Roll out the almond paste to an 18cm (7in) circle, then set aside. Measure the butter, sugar, eggs, flour, baking powder and spices into a bowl and beat until thoroughly blended. Fold in the toasted flaked almonds.

Step three Spoon half the cake mixture into the prepared cake tin and level the surface. Lightly place the circle of almond paste on top, then add the remaining cake mixture and level the surface.

Step four Bake for 1–1¼ hours or until well risen and golden brown and the surface springs back when lightly pressed with a finger. Leave to cool in the tin for 5 minutes then turn out, peel off the parchment and finish cooling on a wire rack.

Step five To make the topping, heat the butter, sugar and cream in a saucepan until blended, then bring to the boil. Stand the wire rack on a baking sheet to catch any drips, then drizzle the topping over the cake. Sprinkle with the toasted flaked almonds, then leave to set for 10–15 minutes.

To make almond paste (this makes approximately 675g/1½lb), mix 225g (8oz) ground almonds with 225g (8oz) caster sugar in a bowl. Add the yolks of 4 large eggs or 2 whole large eggs and 6 drops of almond extract. Knead together to form a stiff paste. Be careful not to over-knead as this will make the paste oily. Wrap in clingfilm and store in the fridge until required.

Cake tin needed:
a deep, round 18cm (7in) cake tin

100g (4oz) almond paste or marzipan

175g (6oz) butter, softened

175g (6oz) caster sugar

3 large eggs

225g (8oz) self-raising flour

2 level tsp baking powder

½ level tsp ground cinnamon

¼ level tsp ground cloves

75g (3oz) toasted flaked almonds

for the topping

50g (2oz) butter

100g (4oz) light muscovado sugar

2 tbsp pouring double cream

25g (1oz) toasted flaked almonds, to sprinkle

Apple and Cinnamon Cake

This is the sort of cake that you would expect to find in a first-class coffee shop or tearoom. It's great for school fêtes and charity events – sell it in wedges, ideally warmed and with dollop of clotted cream.

Cake tin needed:
a deep, round 23cm (9in) cake tin

225g (8oz) butter, softened

225g (8oz) light muscovado sugar

3 large eggs

100g (4oz) chopped walnuts

100g (4oz) sultanas

225g (8oz) self-raising flour

2 level tsp baking powder

400g (14oz) cooking apples, peeled, cored and grated

1 level tsp ground cinnamon

to finish

light muscovado sugar, for sprinkling

extra chopped walnuts, for sprinkling

icing sugar, for dusting

Step one Preheat the oven to 180°C/Fan 160°C/gas 4. Grease the tin, then line the base with non-stick baking parchment.

Step two Measure the butter, sugar, eggs, chopped walnuts, sultanas, flour and baking powder into a large bowl and beat for about 2 minutes until thoroughly blended.

Step three Spoon half the mixture into the prepared tin then spread the grated apple and ground cinnamon in an even layer on top. Spoon the remaining cake mixture on top, level the surface then sprinkle generously with light muscovado sugar and walnuts.

Step four Bake for 1¼–1½ hours or until the cake is well risen and golden brown. Leave to cool in the tin for a few minutes then turn out, peel off the parchment and finish cooling on a wire rack. Dust with icing sugar to serve.

For Mary Berry's baking tips, go to
www.mykitchentable.co.uk/authors/MaryBerry/bakingtips

Madeira Cake

This is a rich, densely textured sponge cake. It is essential that the butter is a creamy spreading consistency before the ingredients are mixed together.

Step one Preheat the oven to 180°C/Fan 160°C/gas 4. Grease the tin and line the base with non-stick baking parchment.

Step two Measure the butter, sugar, flour, ground almonds, eggs and lemon zest into a large bowl. Beat for 1 minute to mix thoroughly. Turn into the prepared tin and level the surface.

Step three Bake for 30 minutes. Place the slice of citron peel on top of the cake and continue cooking for a further 30–45 minutes or until a skewer inserted into the centre comes out clean. Leave to cool in the tin for 10 minutes then turn out, peel off the parchment and finish cooling on a wire rack.

If a fruit or Madeira cake has a slight dip in the centre when it comes out of the oven, turn it out onto non-stick baking parchment on a cooling rack upside down. The action of gravity and the weight of the cake will level the top while it cools.

Cake tin needed:
a deep, round 18cm (7in) cake tin

175g (6oz) butter, softened

175g (6oz) caster sugar

225g (8oz) self-raising flour

50g (2oz) ground almonds

3 large eggs

zest of 1 lemon

a thin slice of citron peel

American Apple and Apricot Cake

This is a new version of a cake that has been a favourite with my family for many years. It can be served with coffee or as a dessert, and is best eaten warm.

Cake tin needed:
a deep, round, loose-based 20cm (8in) cake tin

250g (9oz) self-raising flour

1 level tsp baking powder

225g (8oz) caster sugar

2 large eggs

½ tsp almond extract

150g (5oz) butter, melted

225g (8oz) cooking apples, peeled, cored and thickly sliced

100g (4oz) ready-to-eat dried apricots, snipped into pieces

25g (1oz) flaked almonds

Step one Preheat the oven to 160°C/Fan 140°C/gas 3. Lightly grease the tin and line the base with a circle of non-stick baking parchment.

Step two Measure the flour, baking powder, sugar, eggs, almond extract and melted butter into a large bowl. Mix well to combine, then beat well for 1 minute. Add the apples and apricots to the bowl and gently mix them in.

Step three Spoon the mixture into the prepared tin, gently level the surface and sprinkle with the flaked almonds.

Step four Bake for 1–1½ hours, until the cake is golden, firm to the touch and beginning to shrink away from the side of the tin. Allow to cool in the tin for a few minutes, then turn out onto a plate to serve.

Australian Apple and Raisin Cake

This cake is made with no eggs – useful for those who have an allergy to them. The stewed apple does not have to be a smooth purée – chunks of apple are good in this cake.

Step one Preheat the oven to 160°C/Fan 140°C/gas 3. Lightly grease the tin and line the base with a circle of non-stick baking parchment.

Step two Put the apple slices into a small pan, add a very little water and cook gently until tender. Stir the apple mixture to break it down a little, but it doesn't need to be a smooth purée. Remove from the heat and leave until just warm.

Step three Put the butter and sugar into a large bowl and beat together until evenly blended. Mix together the warm apple and the bicarbonate of soda in a small bowl (the mixture will froth up, but don't worry: this is quite normal). Add to the butter and sugar and stir to mix.

Step four Sift the flour, cocoa powder, nutmeg and cinnamon into the mixture, add the raisins and fold in gently, using a plastic spatula or a large metal spoon. Turn into the prepared cake tin and gently level the surface with a spatula or the back of a spoon.

Step five Bake for 50–60 minutes, until the cake is golden brown in colour, springy to the touch and has begun to shrink away from the side of the tin. Allow to cool in the tin for 5–10 minutes, then turn out, peel off the parchment and leave on a wire rack to cool completely. Dust lightly with icing sugar before serving.

Cake tin needed:
a deep, round, loose-based 18cm (7in) cake tin

1 large cooking apple, peeled, cored and thickly sliced

100g (4oz) butter, softened

100g (4oz) light muscovado sugar

1 level tsp bicarbonate of soda

175g (6oz) self-raising flour

1 level tsp cocoa powder

½ tsp freshly grated nutmeg

½ level tsp ground cinnamon

75g (3oz) raisins

a little icing sugar for dusting

Old-fashioned Seed Cake

You either love or loathe seed cake – this one has a lovely buttery flavour.

Cake tin needed:
a deep, round 18cm
(7in) cake tin

225g (8oz) self-raising
flour

1 level tsp baking
powder

150g (5oz) butter,
softened

150g (5oz) caster
sugar

2 large eggs

2 tbsp milk

50g (2oz) chopped
candied peel

2 level tsp caraway
seeds

Step one Preheat the oven to 180°C/Fan 160°C/gas 4. Grease the cake tin and line the base with non-stick baking parchment.

Step two Measure all the ingredients except the candied peel and caraway seeds into a large bowl. Beat for about 1 minute until thoroughly blended. Carefully fold in the candied peel and caraway seeds, reserving a few seeds to sprinkle over the cake.

Step three Turn the mixture into the prepared tin and sprinkle over the reserved seeds. Bake for about 1 hour, or until well-risen and golden brown and a skewer inserted into the centre comes out clean.

Step four Leave to cool in the tin for 10 minutes then turn out, peel off the parchment and finish cooling on a wire rack.

Have you made this recipe? Tell us what you think at
www.mykitchentable.co.uk/blog

KITCHEN
TABLE

44

Lemon Yoghurt Cake

This is a nice moist cake. Keep in the fridge and eat it within a week.

Step one Preheat the oven to 180°/Fan 160°C/gas 4. Grease the cake tin and line the base with non-stick baking parchment.

Step two Beat together the sugar, butter and egg yolks in a bowl. Add the yoghurt and lemon zest and beat until smooth. Gently fold in the flour.

Step three Whisk the egg whites to a soft peak and carefully fold into the mixture. Turn into the prepared tin.

Step four Bake for 1–1¼ hours or until the cake is well risen and firm to the touch. Leave to cool in the tin for a few minutes then turn out, peel off the parchment and finish cooling on a wire rack.

Step five To make the icing, mix together the sifted icing sugar and the lemon juice. Pour over the cold cake, smooth over with a palette knife and leave to set.

Cake tin needed:
a deep, round 20cm (8in) cake tin

300g (11oz) caster sugar

50g (2oz) butter, softened

3 large eggs, separated

225g (8oz) Greek-style yoghurt

zest of 1 lemon

175g (6oz) self-raising flour

for the icing

100g (4oz) sifted icing sugar

about 1½ tbsp lemon juice

Iced Fairy Cakes

This makes special little cakes, ideal for children's parties.

Makes 12

Cake tin needed:
a 12-hole bun tin

100g (4oz) butter, softened

100g (4oz) caster sugar

2 large eggs

100g (4oz) self-raising flour

1 level tsp baking powder

for the icing

225g (8oz) sifted icing sugar

2–3 tbsp warm water

sweets, to decorate

Step one Preheat the oven to 200°C/Fan 180°C/gas 6. Place fairy cake cases into the bun tin, so that the cakes keep a good even shape as they bake.

Step two Measure all the cake ingredients into a large bowl and beat for 2–3 minutes until the mixture is well blended and smooth. Fill each paper case with the mixture.

Step three Bake for 15–20 minutes or until the cakes are well risen and golden brown. Lift the paper cases out of the bun tin and cool the cakes on a wire rack.

Step four To make the icing, put the icing sugar in a bowl and gradually blend in the warm water until you have a fairly stiff icing. Spoon over the top of the cakes and decorate with sweets, then leave to set.

To make Orange Fairy Cakes, follow the recipe above and add the zest of 1 orange in step 2. To make the icing, gradually blend 225g (8oz) sifted icing sugar with the juice of 1 orange until you have a fairly stiff icing. Spoon over the tops of the cakes.

Butterfly Cakes

Butterfly cakes are quick and easy to make, and very effective for a children's party.

Step one Preheat the oven to 200°C/Fan 180°C/gas 6. Place fairy cake cases into the bun tin, so that the cakes keep a good even shape as they bake.

Step two Measure all the cake ingredients into a large bowl and beat well for 2–3 minutes until the mixture is well blended and smooth. Fill each paper case with the mixture.

Step three Bake for 15–20 minutes or until the cakes are well risen and golden brown. Lift the paper cases out of the bun tin and cool the cakes on a wire rack.

Step four To make the icing, beat the butter and icing sugar together until well blended. Cut a slice from the top of each cake and cut this slice in half. Pipe a swirl of butter cream into the centre of each cake and place the half slices of cake on top to resemble butterfly wings. Dust the cakes with icing sugar to finish.

To make Chocolate Butterfly Cakes, follow the recipe above, then make chocolate icing by mixing 2 tablespoons of cocoa powder with 3 tablespoons of hot water. Allow to cool slightly, then beat in 175g (6oz) softened butter and 350g (12oz) sifted icing sugar until well blended. To make these butterfly cakes really chocolaty, you can replace 25g (1oz) of self-raising flour from the cake ingredients with 25g (1oz) cocoa powder to make the cakes have a chocolate flavour too.

To make Orange or Lemon Butterfly Cakes, add the zest of 1 orange or lemon to the cake mixture in step 2. Ice them with a butter cream made from butter, icing sugar and a little orange or lemon juice, then dust with icing sugar.

Makes 12

Cake tin needed:
a 12-hole bun tin

100g (4oz) butter, softened

100g (4oz) caster sugar

2 large eggs

100g (4oz) self-raising flour

1 level tsp baking powder

for the icing

175g (6oz) butter, softened

350g (12oz) sifted icing sugar, plus extra for dusting

Cupcakes

Cupcakes are great for teatime, or arranged stacked on a cake stand instead of a large traditional birthday cake or even a wedding cake. Cupcakes are a different shape to fairy cakes – the cases they are baked in are deeper and have less angular sides.

Makes 12

Cake tin needed:
a 12-hole muffin tin

100g (4oz) butter, softened

150g (5oz) self-raising flour

150g (5oz) caster sugar

3 tbsp milk

2 large eggs

½ tsp vanilla extract

for the butter icing

100g (4oz) butter, softened

225g (8oz) sifted icing sugar

½ tsp vanilla extract

to decorate

plain or white chocolate curls or shavings

silver hearts, 100s and 1000s, silver balls and coloured sweets

Step one Preheat the oven to 180°C/Fan 160°C/gas 4. Put the muffin cases into the muffin tin, so that the cakes keep a good even shape as they bake.

Step two Measure all the cupcake ingredients into a large bowl and beat until blended and smooth. Spoon evenly between the paper cases.

Step three Bake for 20–25 minutes or until risen and golden brown. Lift the paper cases out of the tin and cool the cakes on a wire rack until completely cold before icing.

Step four To make the butter icing, beat together all the icing ingredients to give a creamy thick icing, then smooth over the cold cupcakes. If decorating with chocolate curls, allow the chocolate bar to reach room temperature then shave using a vegetable peeler.

If you are making a double quantity of cupcakes or are using a smaller tin, you can prepare your cupcake mixture in one go and spoon it into the paper cases ready to go into the oven. They will come to no harm, as raising agents react more slowly nowadays. Bake only one tray of cupcakes at a time though.

To make chocolate or coffee icing, add 2 tbsp of cocoa powder or 1 tsp of coffee essence to the butter icing.

Chocolate Brownies

The best brownies are soft in the centre and have a crust on top. This recipe couldn't be simpler – all you do is measure the ingredients into a bowl and give it all a good mix!

Step one Preheat the oven to 180°C/Fan 160°C/gas 4. Cut a rectangle of non-stick baking parchment to fit the base and sides of the tin. Grease the tin and then line it with the paper, pushing it neatly into the corners.

Step two Measure all the ingredients into a large bowl and mix with a hand-held electric mixer until evenly blended.

Step three Spoon the mixture into the prepared tin, scraping the sides of the bowl with a plastic spatula to remove all of it. Spread the mixture gently to the corners of the tin and level the surface with the back of the spatula.

Step four Bake for 40–45 minutes, until the brownies have a crusty top and a skewer inserted into the centre comes out clean. Cover loosely with foil for the last 10 minutes if the mixture is browning too much. Allow the brownies to cool in the tin and then cut into 24 squares. Store in an airtight tin.

Makes 24

Cake tin needed:
a 30 x 23 x 4cm
(12 x 9 x 1½ in)
traybake tin or
roasting tin

275g (10oz) butter,
softened

375g (13oz) caster
sugar

4 large eggs

75g (3oz) cocoa
powder

100g (4oz) self-raising
flour

100g (4oz) plain
chocolate chips

For step-by-step photographs of this recipe, go to
www.mykitchentable.co.uk/recipes/chocolatebrownies

Dark Indulgent Chocolate and Walnut Brownies

With a little coffee, some chopped walnuts and the addition of plain chocolate chips, these brownies have a rich, 'grown-up' flavour. Cooked brownie mixture, like gingerbread, is likely to dip in the middle, but this all adds to the charm!

Makes 24

Cake tin needed:
a 30 x 23cm (12 x 9in) traybake or roasting tin

350g (12oz) plain chocolate (39 per cent cocoa solids)

225g (8oz) butter

2 level tsp instant coffee powder

2 tbsp hot water

3 large eggs

225g (8oz) caster sugar

1 tsp vanilla extract

75g (3oz) self-raising flour

175g (6oz) chopped walnuts

225g (8oz) plain chocolate chips

Step one Preheat the oven to 190°C/Fan 170°C/gas 5. Grease the tin then line the base with non-stick baking parchment.

Step two Break up the chocolate into pieces and melt slowly with the butter in a bowl set over a pan of hot water, stirring occasionally. Leave to cool. Dissolve the coffee in the hot water.

Step three In another bowl, mix together the coffee, eggs, sugar and vanilla extract. Gradually beat in the chocolate mixture. Fold in the flour, walnuts and chocolate chips, and then pour the mixture into the prepared tin.

Step four Bake for 40–45 minutes or until the brownies have a crusty top and a skewer inserted into the centre comes out clean. Leave the brownies to cool in the tin and then cut into 24 squares. Store in an airtight tin.

Blueberry Muffins

Best served warm, these are wonderful for breakfast. Don't expect them to be sweet like a cake – they are more like scones. Paper muffin cases are not essential but they do make life easier when extracting the muffins from the tin!

Step one Preheat the oven to 200°C/Fan 180°C/gas 6. Grease the muffin tins, or put a paper muffin case into each muffin 'hole' or on a baking sheet.

Step two Measure the flour, baking powder, sugar and grated lemon zest into a mixing bowl and stir briefly to combine.

Step three Mix together the eggs, milk, cooled melted butter and vanilla extract and then add these to the dry ingredients. Mix quickly but gently to blend the ingredients together. Don't overmix; it doesn't need to be a smooth mixture, as long as the dry ingredients are incorporated. Gently stir in the blueberries.

Step four Spoon the mixture into the muffin tin, filling each hole or case almost to the top. Bake for 20–25 minutes, until well risen, golden and firm to the touch. Allow to cool for a few minutes in the tin, then lift out and cool for a little longer on a wire rack. Serve warm.

If you have made the muffins ahead and want to reheat them, pop them in a low oven for a few minutes.

Makes 12

Cake tin needed:
a deep, 12-hole muffin tin

275g (10oz) plain flour

1 level tsp baking powder

75g (3oz) caster sugar

zest of 1 lemon

2 large eggs

225ml (8fl oz) milk

100g (4oz) butter, melted and cooled

½ tsp vanilla extract

225g (8oz) blueberries

Chocolate Chip American Muffins

These large muffins look quite impressive. They're best eaten on the day of baking.

Makes 12

Cake tin needed:
a 12-hole muffin tin

250g (9oz) self-raising flour

1 level tsp baking powder

50g (2oz) butter, softened

75g (3oz) caster sugar

175g (6oz) plain chocolate chips

2 large eggs

1 tsp vanilla extract

250ml (9fl oz) milk

Step one Preheat the oven to 200°C/Fan 180°C/gas 6. Place muffin cases into the muffin tin.

Step two Measure the flour and baking powder into a large bowl, then add the butter and rub into the flour until the mixture resembles fine breadcrumbs. Stir in the sugar and chocolate chips.

Step three Mix together the eggs, vanilla extract and milk, then pour the mixture all in one go into the dry ingredients. Mix quickly with a wooden spoon to blend. The mixture should have a lumpy consistency. Spoon the mixture into the paper cases in the tin, filling almost to the top.

Step four Bake for 20–25 minutes or until well risen and firm to the touch. Leave to cool for a few minutes in the tray, then lift out the paper cases and cool the muffins for a little longer on a wire rack.

Mini St Clements Muffins

These are not breakfast muffins and are therefore sweeter. They are delicious at any time and children love them, too. It is easier to use small paper cases to line the mini-muffin tins. If you don't have any cases, grease the tins well and leave the muffins to cool before trying to remove them – if you try to remove them when they are hot, they tend to come apart!

Step one Preheat the oven to 200°C/Fan 180°C/gas 6. Line the mini-muffin tins with paper cases.

Step two Cut the whole orange into chunks and remove any pips with the point of a knife. Process the orange in a food processor until finely chopped.

Step three Put all the remaining ingredients except the icing sugar into a mixing bowl and beat quickly with a wooden spoon until just mixed. Gently stir in the chopped orange.

Step four Spoon the mixture into the cases, filling them almost to the top. Bake for about 15 minutes, until well risen, golden and firm to the touch. Lift the paper cases out of the tin. Dust with icing sugar and serve while still warm.

Makes about 24

Cake tins needed:
2 x 12-hole mini-muffin tins

1 thin-skinned orange, washed

zest of 1 lemon

100g (4oz) caster sugar

1 large egg

100ml (3½ fl oz) milk

50g (2oz) butter, melted and slightly cooled

1 level tsp baking powder

175g (6oz) self-raising flour

icing sugar, for dusting

Mini Jammy Cakes

These are usually made with the jam enclosed, but here they are left open so that the jam becomes nice and chewy. The cakes are best served warm.

Makes 24

**Cake tins needed:
2 baking sheets**

225g (8oz) self-raising
flour

¼ level tsp ground
mixed spice

50g (2oz) butter,
softened

100g (4oz) caster
sugar

1 large egg, beaten

3–4 tbsp milk

a little blackcurrant
jam

a little granulated
sugar, for sprinkling

Step one Preheat the oven to 200°C/Fan 180°C/gas 6. Lightly grease the baking sheets.

Step two Measure the flour, spice and butter into a bowl and rub in the butter with your fingertips until the mixture resembles fine breadcrumbs. Stir in the sugar.

Step three Mix the egg and milk together and stir into the mixture, adding only enough of the liquid to make a stiff dough. Divide the dough into about 24 pieces and roll each piece into a smooth ball.

Step four Using the handle of a wooden spoon, make a hole in the centre of each ball of dough and put about ¼ tsp jam into each one. Place the balls of dough – jam side up – onto the prepared baking sheets and sprinkle them with a little granulated sugar.

Step five Bake for about 10 minutes until the cakes are a pale golden brown. Lift them off the tray and allow to cool a little on a wire rack. Serve still warm.

Little Gems

Children love to help by putting their favourite sweets on top of these tiny cakes. This recipe makes 65 gems, which sounds like a lot, but they are very tiny as they are made in sweetie or petits fours cases.

Step one Preheat the oven to 180°C/Fan 160°C/gas 4. Arrange about 65 petits fours cases on the baking sheets.

Step two Measure all the cake ingredients into a bowl and beat well until thoroughly blended. Spoon scant teaspoonfuls of the mixture into the cases, being careful not to overfill.

Step three Bake for 15–20 minutes until well risen and pale golden brown. Cool on a wire rack.

Step four To make the icing, measure the icing sugar into a bowl and add enough lemon juice to give a spreading consistency. Spoon a little on top of each cooled gem and spread out with the back of a teaspoon. When the icing has almost set, top with a sweet.

Makes 65

Cake tins needed:
2 baking sheets

75g (3oz) butter, softened

2 large eggs

100g (4oz) self-raising flour

1 level tsp baking powder

75g (3oz) caster sugar

1 tbsp milk

for the icing

100g (4oz) sifted icing sugar

about 1 tbsp lemon juice

small sweets, to decorate

Fast Flapjacks

These flapjacks are crunchy and traditional. Take care not to overbake them, as they can become hard and dark.

Makes 24

Cake tin needed:
a 30 x 23cm (12 x 9in) traybake or roasting tin

225g (8oz) butter

225g (8oz) demerara sugar

75g (3oz) golden syrup

275g (10oz) porridge oats

Step one Preheat the oven to 160°C/Fan 140°C/gas 3. Grease the tin.

Step two Melt the butter in a large pan along with the sugar and syrup, and then stir in the oats. Mix well and then turn into the prepared tin and press flat with a palette knife or the back of a spoon.

Step three Bake for about 35 minutes or until pale golden brown. Remove from the oven and leave to cool for 10 minutes. Mark into 24 squares and leave to finish cooling in the tin.

To make Chocolate Chip Flapjacks (in photo), leave the mixture to cool, after stirring in the oats in step 2. Stir in 100g (4oz) plain chocolate chips, then turn into the prepared tin and follow the remainder of the method for the above recipe.

To make Muesli Flapjacks, replace 175g (6oz) of the porridge oats with your favourite muesli, then follow the recipe above. Leave to cool for 10 minutes, then mark into 16 oblongs and leave to finish cooling in the tin. If you like a lot of raisins add 25–50g (1–2oz) extra when you make the flapjack mixture.

Apricot Swiss Cakes

Traditionally a red jam is used for the centre of these cakes, which are buttery and very delicious but apricot jam makes a lovely alternative.

Makes 12

Cake tin needed:
a 12-hole bun tin

225g (8oz) butter

75g (3oz) sifted icing sugar

200g (7oz) self-raising flour

50g (2oz) cornflour

to finish

a little apricot jam

icing sugar, for dusting

Step one Preheat the oven to 180°C/Fan 160°C/gas 4. Place fairy cake cases into the bun tin.

Step two Soften the butter in a large bowl. Add the icing sugar and beat well until really soft and fluffy. Stir in the flours and mix until smooth. Spoon the mixture into a large piping bag fitted with a large star nozzle. Pipe circles of the mixture into the base of each paper case until all the mixture is used up.

Step three Bake for 15–20 minutes or until pale golden brown. Remove the paper cases from the tin and cool the cakes on a wire rack.

Step four Put a small amount of apricot jam onto the centre of each cake. Dust lightly with sifted icing sugar.

The Very Best Shortbread

For a really good shortbread it is essential to use butter. I like to use semolina as well as flour to give the shortbread crunch, but you can use cornflour or ground rice instead.

Makes 30 fingers

Cake tin needed:
a 30 x 23cm (12 x 9in)
traybake or roasting
tin

225g (8oz) plain flour

100g (4oz) semolina

225g (8oz) butter

100g (4oz) caster
sugar

50g (2oz) flaked
almonds (optional)

25g (1oz) demerara
sugar, for dusting

Step one Preheat the oven to 160°C/Fan 140°C/gas 3. Lightly grease the tin.

Step two Mix together the flour and semolina in a bowl or food processor. Add the butter and sugar and rub together with your fingertips until the mixture is just beginning to bind together. Knead lightly until the mixture forms a smooth dough.

Step three Press the dough into the prepared tin and level it with the back of a spatula or a palette knife, making sure the mixture is evenly spread. Prick all over with a fork, sprinkle over the flaked almonds if using, and chill until firm.

Step four Bake for about 35 minutes or until a very pale golden brown. Sprinkle with demerara sugar and leave to cool in the tin for a few minutes, then cut into 30 fingers. Carefully lift the fingers out of the tin with a palette knife and finish cooling on a wire rack. Store in an airtight tin.

To make Orange Shortbread, add the zest of one large orange to the mixture.

Glacé cherries, dried apricots and sultanas make delicious additions to shortbread, but the biscuits then need to be eaten on the day of making as they soon become soggy with the moisture from the fruit.

KITCHEN TABLE

Have you made this recipe? Tell us what you think at
www.mykitchentable.co.uk/blog

Coffee and Walnut Traybake

Coffee and walnuts go particularly well together, but you can use other nuts for this recipe if you prefer.

Step one Preheat the oven to 180°C/Fan 160°C/gas 4. Grease the tin then line the base with non-stick baking parchment.

Step two Measure all the cake ingredients into a large bowl and beat until well blended. Turn the mixture into the prepared tin and level the surface.

Step three Bake for 35–40 minutes or until the cake has shrunk from the sides of the tin and springs back when pressed in the centre with your fingertips. Leave to cool in the tin.

Step four To make the icing, beat together the butter, icing sugar, milk and coffee essence. Spread evenly over the cold cake using a palette knife, then decorate with the walnut halves and cut into pieces.

If you like, you can use instant coffee powder instead of coffee essence: mix 2 tsp with 2 tbsp of water.

Makes 12 squares

Cake tin needed:
a 30 x 23cm (12 x 9in) traybake or roasting tin

225g (8oz) butter, softened

225g (8oz) light muscovado sugar

275g (10oz) self-raising flour

2 level tsp baking powder

4 large eggs

2 tbsp milk

2 tbsp coffee essence

75g (3oz) chopped walnuts

for the icing

75g (3oz) butter, softened

225g (8oz) sifted icing sugar

2 tsp milk

2 tsp coffee essence

walnut halves

Cherry and Almond Traybake

In season, you can use fresh stoned cherries instead of glacé, but you must then eat the cake up quickly: it won't keep as well because it will be moister.

Makes 12 squares

Cake tin needed: a 30 x 23cm (12 x 9in) traybake or roasting tin

225g (8oz) red or natural glacé cherries (or 450g/1lb of sweet black cherries, stoned)

275g (10oz) self-raising flour

2 level tsp baking powder

225g (8oz) butter, softened

225g (8oz) caster sugar

zest of 2 lemons

75g (3oz) ground almonds

5 large eggs

25g (1oz) flaked almonds

Step one Preheat the oven to 180°C/Fan 160°C/gas 4. Grease the tin then line the base with non-stick baking parchment.

Step two Cut the cherries into quarters, put them in a sieve and rinse under running water. Drain well then dry thoroughly with kitchen paper.

Step three Measure all the remaining cake ingredients, except the flaked almonds, into a large bowl and beat for 1 minute to mix thoroughly. Lightly fold in the cherries. Turn into the prepared tin and sprinkle over the flaked almonds.

Step four Bake for about 40 minutes or until the cake has shrunk from the sides of the tin and springs back when pressed in the centre with your fingertips. Leave to cool in the tin, then cut into pieces.

For Mary Berry's tips on how to line a baking tin, go to
www.mykitchentable.co.uk/authors/MaryBerry/liningtins

KITCHEN TABLE

Ginger and Treacle Spiced Traybake

Treacle can be difficult to weigh accurately, as it tends to stick to the scale pan. Weighing it on top of the sugar overcomes this problem.

Step one Preheat the oven to 180°C/Fan 160°C/gas 4. Grease the tin then line the base with non-stick baking parchment.

Step two Measure all the ingredients for the traybake into a large bowl and beat until well blended. Turn the mixture into the prepared tin, scraping the bowl with a plastic spatula to remove all the mixture. Level the surface gently with the back of the spatula.

Step three Bake for 35–40 minutes, or until the cake has shrunk from the sides of the tin and springs back when pressed in the centre with your fingertips. Leave to cool in the tin for a few minutes then turn out, peel off the parchment and finish cooling on a wire rack.

Step four To make the icing, sift the icing sugar into a bowl, add the ginger syrup and mix until the icing is smooth and has a spreading consistency. Pour the icing over the cake, spread it gently to the edges with a small palette knife and sprinkle with the chopped stem ginger to decorate. Allow the icing to set before slicing the traybake into pieces.

This traybake freezes very well un-iced, and in fact improves with freezing.

Makes 15–20 pieces

Cake tin needed:
a 30 x 23cm (12 x 9in) traybake or roasting tin

225g (8oz) butter, softened

175g (6oz) light muscovado sugar

200g (7oz) black treacle

300g (11oz) self-raising flour

2 level tsp baking powder

1 level tsp ground mixed spice

1 level tsp ground allspice

4 large eggs

4 tbsp milk

3 bulbs of stem ginger from a jar, finely chopped

for the icing

75g (3oz) icing sugar

3 tbsp stem ginger syrup from the jar

3 bulbs of stem ginger from a jar, finely chopped, to decorate

Banana and Honey Teabread

This teabread has quite a pale colour even when cooked, because of the thick pale honey used. It is a very good way of using up over-ripe bananas.

Cake tin needed:
a 900g (2lb) loaf tin

225g (8oz) self-raising flour

¼ level tsp freshly grated nutmeg

100g (4oz) butter

225g (8oz) bananas

100g (4oz) caster sugar

zest of 1 lemon

2 large eggs

6 tbsp thick pale honey

for the topping

2 tbsp honey

nibbed sugar or crushed sugar cubes, for sprinkling

Step one Preheat the oven to 160°C/Fan 140°C/gas 3. Grease the tin then line the base with non-stick baking parchment.

Step two Measure the flour and nutmeg into a large bowl and then rub in the butter using your fingertips, until the mixture resembles fine breadcrumbs.

Step three Peel and mash the bananas and stir into the flour mixture, along with the sugar, lemon zest, eggs and honey. Beat well until evenly mixed, then turn into the prepared tin and level the surface.

Step four Bake for about 1¼ hours or until a fine skewer inserted into the centre comes out clean. Cover the teabread loosely with foil during the end of the cooking time if it is browning too much. Leave to cool in the tin for a few minutes then turn out, peel off the parchment and finish cooling on a wire rack.

Step five To make the topping, gently warm the honey in a small pan, then brush over the top of the cold teabread. Sprinkle with the nibbed sugar.

Pineapple and Cherry Loaf

This cake would make a lovely present for someone with a sweet tooth. Remember that it is important to keep it in the fridge as it is very moist, and could go mouldy if left in a tin in a warm kitchen.

Step one Preheat the oven to 160°C/Fan 140°C/gas 3. Grease the tin then line the base with non-stick baking parchment.

Step two Cut the cherries into quarters, put in a sieve and rinse under running water. Drain well. Drain the pineapple, reserving 2 tbsp of juice, and roughly chop; dry the pineapple and cherries thoroughly with kitchen paper.

Step three Measure the softened butter, sugar, eggs and flour into a large mixing bowl and beat for about 2 minutes until smooth. Fold in the sultanas, pineapple and cherries, along with the reserved pineapple juice. Turn into the prepared loaf tin.

Step four Bake for 1¼–1½ hours or until the loaf is well risen, golden brown and shrinking slightly from the sides of the tin. Leave to cool in the tin for a few minutes then turn out, peel off the parchment and finish cooling on a wire rack. Store in an airtight container in the fridge.

Cake tin needed:
a 900g (2lb) loaf tin

175g (6oz) red or natural glacé cherries

227g (8oz) tin pineapple rings or chunks in fruit juice

150g (5oz) butter, softened

100g (4oz) light muscovado sugar

2 large eggs, beaten

200g (7oz) self-raising flour

225g (8oz) sultanas

Lemon Drizzle Traybake

This really is our top favourite. It is always moist and crunchy. The cake needs to be still warm when the topping is added so that it absorbs the lemon syrup easily, leaving the sugar on top. Do allow the cake to cool a little though – if it is too hot, the syrup will tend to run straight through.

Makes 30 squares

Cake tin needed:
a 30 x 23 x 4cm (12 x 9 x 1½ in) traybake or roasting tin

225g (8oz) butter, softened

225g (8oz) caster sugar

275g (10oz) self-raising flour

2 level tsp baking powder

4 large eggs

4 tbsp milk

finely grated zest of 2 lemons

for the crunchy topping

175g (6oz) granulated sugar

juice of 2 lemons

Step one Preheat the oven to 160°C/Fan 140°C/gas 3. Cut a rectangle of non-stick baking parchment to fit the tin. Grease the tin and then line with the paper, pushing it neatly into the corners.

Step two Measure all the ingredients for the traybake into a large bowl and beat well for about 2 minutes, until well blended. Turn the mixture into the prepared tin, scraping the sides of the bowl with a plastic spatula to remove all of the mixture. Level the surface gently with the back of the spatula.

Step three Bake for 35–40 minutes, until the traybake springs back when pressed lightly with a finger in the centre and is beginning to shrink away from the sides of the tin. Allow to cool in the tin for a few minutes, then lift the cake out of the tin still in the lining paper. Carefully remove the paper and put the cake onto a wire rack placed over a tray (to catch drips of the topping).

Step four To make the crunchy topping, mix the granulated sugar and lemon juice in a small bowl to give a runny consistency. Spoon this mixture evenly over the traybake while it is still just warm. Leave to cool completely before cutting into pieces.

Borrowdale Teabread

A wonderful moist teabread to serve buttered. The fruit is soaked in tea overnight. You can make two 450g (1lb) loaves from this recipe instead of one large loaf, but reduce the cooking time to 30–40 minutes.

Step one Put the sultanas, currants and raisins in a bowl and pour in the tea. Cover and leave to soak overnight.

Step two Preheat the oven to 180°C/Fan 160°C/gas 4. Grease the tin then line the base with non-stick baking parchment.

Step three Mix the sugar and eggs together until light and fluffy. Add the flour along with the soaked fruits and any left-over liquid, and mix together thoroughly. Spoon the mixture into the prepared loaf tin and level the surface.

Step four Bake for about 1 hour or until a skewer inserted into the centre comes out clean. Leave to cool in the tin. Serve sliced and spread with butter.

Cake tin needed:
a 900g (2lb) loaf tin

100g (4oz) sultanas

100g (4oz) currants

100g (4oz) raisins

475ml (16fl oz) strong tea, strained

225g (8oz) light muscovado sugar

2 large eggs

450g (1lb) wholemeal self-raising flour

Pineapple and Sultana Cake

A lovely moist cake, but do make sure that you dry the pineapple thoroughly. The cake will keep for up to a month in an airtight container in the fridge.

Cake tin needed:
a deep, round 20cm
(8in) cake tin

225g (8oz) tin
pineapple rings or
chunks in fruit juice

50g (2oz) glacé
cherries

150g (5oz) butter,
softened

120g (4½ oz) light
muscovado sugar

2 large eggs

200g (7oz) self-raising
flour

350g (12oz) sultanas

Step one Preheat the oven to 160°C/Fan 140°C/gas 3. Grease the cake tin and line the base and sides with non-stick baking parchment.

Step two Drain the pineapple, reserving 2 tbsp of the juice. Dry the pineapple thoroughly with kitchen paper then chop finely. Quarter the cherries then rinse and dry thoroughly.

Step three Measure the butter, sugar, eggs and flour into a mixing bowl. Mix together until thoroughly blended, smooth and glossy. Fold in the pineapple, cherries and sultanas and the reserved pineapple juice. Turn into the prepared cake tin.

Step four Bake for 1¼–1½ hours or until the cake is a pale golden brown, firm to the touch and shrinking away from the sides of the tin. Leave to cool in the tin, then peel off the baking parchment.

Iced Apricot Fruit Loaf

Like any fruit loaf, this is easy to make. I've found it to be a popular choice at fêtes and charity events, sold in slices or whole.

Step one Preheat the oven to 160°C/fan 140°C/gas 3. Grease the tin then line the base with non-stick baking parchment.

Step two Cut the cherries into quarters, put in a sieve and rinse under running water. Drain well then dry thoroughly with some kitchen paper.

Step three Break the eggs into a large bowl and then measure in the remaining cake ingredients, including the cherries. Beat well until the mixture is smooth. Turn into the prepared tin and level the surface.

Step four Bake for about 1 hour 10 minutes or until the cake is golden brown, firm to the touch and shrinking away from the sides of the tin. A fine skewer inserted into the centre of the loaf should come out clean. Leave to cool in the tin for 10 minutes then turn out, peel off the parchment and finish cooling on a wire rack.

Step five To make the icing, measure the sifted icing sugar into a bowl. Heat the apricot jam and water together until the jam melts then pour onto the icing sugar. Mix to a smooth spreading consistency, then spoon over the top of the cold loaf. Decorate the loaf by sprinkling the chopped apricots down the centre.

Cake tin needed:
a 900g (2lb) loaf tin

75g (3oz) red or natural glacé cherries

3 large eggs

175g (6oz) self-raising flour

100g (4oz) butter, softened

100g (4oz) light muscovado sugar

100g (4oz) ready-to-eat dried apricots, chopped

150g (5oz) sultanas

for the icing

100g (4oz) sifted icing sugar

1 tbsp apricot jam

1 tbsp water

2 ready-to-eat dried apricots, chopped

Have you made this recipe? Tell us what you think at
www.mykitchentable.co.uk/blog

KITCHEN TABLE

Sultana and Orange Traybake

Oranges and sultanas go well together in this cake. Sprinkling the cake with demerara sugar gives it a nice crusty, sugary top.

Makes 21 pieces

Cake tin needed:
a 30 x 23cm (12 x 9in) traybake or roasting tin

225g (8oz) butter, softened

225g (8oz) caster sugar

275g (10oz) self-raising flour

2 level tsp baking powder

4 large eggs

2 tbsp milk

275g (10oz) sultanas

zest of 2 oranges

demerara sugar, for sprinkling

Step one Preheat the oven to 180°C/Fan 160°C/gas 4. Grease the tin then line the base with non-stick baking parchment.

Step two Measure all the cake ingredients except the demerara sugar into a large bowl and beat until well blended. Turn the mixture into the prepared tin and level the surface.

Step three Bake for about 25 minutes then sprinkle the top with demerara sugar and return to the oven for a further 10–15 minutes or until the cake has shrunk from the sides of the tin and springs back when pressed in the centre with your fingertips. Leave to cool in the tin, then cut into pieces.

You can omit the demerara sugar topping and instead ice the cooked and cooled cake with orange glacé icing made with 225g (8oz) sifted icing sugar and about 3 tbsp of freshly squeezed orange juice (as shown in photo).

Date and Chocolate Loaf

A rich loaf that's so moist it doesn't need to be buttered. The dates give the cake a lovely texture and toffee flavour.

Step one Preheat the oven to 180°C/Fan 160°C/gas 4. Grease the tin then line the base with non-stick baking parchment.

Step two Roughly chop the dates and place in a small bowl. Pour over the boiling water and leave to soak for 30 minutes. Break up the chocolate and melt with the butter in a small bowl, set over a pan of simmering water, stirring occasionally. Roughly chop the Brazil nuts and reserve about two tablespoons for decoration.

Step three Mix together the flour, caster sugar, baking powder and bicarbonate of soda. In a separate bowl, mix together the egg and milk and beat this into the dry ingredients, adding the nuts, dates and their soaking liquid, and the chocolate mixture. Spoon into the prepared tin, level the surface and sprinkle over the reserved nuts along with the demerara sugar.

Step four Bake for about 1¼ hours or until a skewer inserted into the centre comes out clean. Cover loosely with foil towards the end of the cooking time if the cake is becoming too brown. Leave to cool in the tin for 10 minutes then turn out, peel off the parchment and finish cooling on a wire rack.

Cake tin needed:
a 900g (2lb) loaf tin

150g (5oz) stoned dried dates

150ml (¼ pint) boiling water

150g (5oz) plain chocolate (39 per cent cocoa solids)

40g (1½ oz) butter, softened

150g (5oz) Brazil nuts

225g (8oz) plain flour

40g (1½ oz) caster sugar

1 level tsp baking powder

1 level tsp bicarbonate of soda

1 large egg

150ml (¼ pint) milk

demerara sugar, for sprinkling

Bakewell Tart Traybake

The origins of the traditional bakewell tart are hotly contested. Here is my version, in which I've turned the tart into an easy-to-make traybake.

Makes 21 squares

Cake tin needed:
a 30 x 23cm (12 x 9in) traybake or roasting tin

4 tbsp raspberry jam

flaked almonds, for sprinkling

for the pastry

175g (6oz) plain flour

85g (3oz) hard butter, dices

for the sponge

115g (4oz) butter, softened

115g (4oz) caster sugar

175g (6oz) self-raising flour

1 level tsp baking powder

2 large eggs

2 tbsp milk

½ tsp almond extract

Step one Preheat the oven to 180°C/Fan 160°C/gas 4.

Step two To make the pastry, measure the flour into a bowl and rub in the butter with your fingers until the mixture resembles fine breadcrumbs. Bind to a dough with two to three tablespoons of cold water. Roll out on a lightly floured surface and line the tin; spread with the jam.

Step three To make the sponge, measure all the ingredients into a large bowl and beat well for 2 minutes or until well blended. Transfer to the tin, level the surface and sprinkle with almonds.

Step four Bake for 25 minutes or until the cake has shrunk from the sides of the tin and springs back when pressed in the centre with your fingertips. Leave to cool in the tin, then cut into squares. Lift out using a palette knife.

Devonshire Apple Cake

This apple cake looks a little unappetizing when cold, but is quite delicious served warm with cream or fromage frais.

Step one Preheat the oven to 180°C/Fan 160°C/gas 4. Grease the tin then line the base with non-stick baking parchment.

Step two Peel, core and thinly slice the apples and squeeze the lemon juice over them. Measure the flour, baking powder and sugar into a large bowl. Beat the eggs together with the almond extract and stir into the flour along with the melted butter. Whisk, then spread half this mixture into the tin. Arrange the apples over the top of the cake mixture. Carefully top with the remainder of the mixture – don't worry if the apples show through a little. Sprinkle over the almonds.

Step three Bake for about 1¼ hours or until the cake is golden, firm to the touch and slightly shrunk away from the sides of the tin. Leave to cool for 15 minutes and then turn out and peel off the parchment. Sprinkle over the caster sugar and serve warm, with cream or fromage frais.

Makes 12 squares

Cake tin needed:
a 30 x 23cm (12 x 9in) traybake or roasting tin

450g (1lb) cooking apples

juice of ½ lemon

350g (12oz) self-raising flour

2 level tsp baking powder

350g (12oz) caster sugar

4 large eggs

1 tsp almond extract

225g (8oz) butter, melted

a generous scattering of shredded, flaked or chopped almonds

caster sugar, for sprinkling

Bara Brith

There are many versions of this traditional teabread. In Welsh, 'bara brith' means 'speckled bread'. Similar breads are made in different parts of Britain, such as Barm Brack in Ireland and Selkirk Bannock in Scotland.

Cake tin needed:
a 900g (2lb) loaf tin

175g (6oz) currants

175g (6oz) sultanas

225g (8oz) light muscovado sugar

300ml (½ pint) strong hot tea

275g (10oz) self-raising flour

1 large egg, beaten

Step one Measure the fruit and sugar into a bowl, pour over the hot tea, cover and leave overnight.

Step two Preheat the oven to 150°C/Fan 130°C/gas 2. Grease the tin then line the base with non-stick baking parchment.

Step three Stir the flour and egg into the fruit mixture, mix thoroughly then turn into the prepared tin and level the surface.

Step four Bake for about 1½ hours or until well risen and firm to the touch. A skewer inserted into the centre should come out clean. Leave to cool in the tin for 10 minutes then turn out, peel off the parchment and finish cooling on a wire rack. Serve sliced and buttered.

Have you made this recipe? Tell us what you think at
www.mykitchentable.co.uk/blog

Sultana Malt Loaves

These can be made in advance as they keep very well and can also be frozen. This recipe makes two loaves.

Step one Preheat the oven to 150°C/Fan 130°C/gas 2. Grease the tins then line the base of each with non-stick baking parchment.

Step two Measure the flour, bicarbonate of soda and baking powder into a bowl and stir in the sultanas. Gently heat the sugar, malt extract and black treacle together. Pour onto the dry ingredients, along with the beaten eggs and the tea. Beat well until smooth. Pour into the prepared tins.

Step three Bake for about 1 hour or until well risen and firm to the touch. Leave to cool in the tins for 10 minutes then turn out, peel off the parchment and finish cooling on a wire rack. These loaves are best kept for 2 days before eating.

Freeze loaves as soon as they are cold. If you want to ice this loaf, leave it until it unfrozen. Some icing loses its sheen in the freezer, so it's usually best to freeze the loaf un-iced. Butter cream icing is an exception.

Cake tins needed:
2 x 450g (1lb) loaf tins

225g (8oz) plain flour

½ level tsp bicarbonate of soda

1 level tsp baking powder

225g (8oz) sultanas

50g (2oz) demerara sugar

175g (6oz) malt extract

1 tbsp black treacle

2 large eggs, beaten

150ml (¼ pint) strained cold black tea

Basic All-in-one Sponge Traybake

This is the simplest of cakes to make. When cooked and cold, sift over a little icing sugar to finish, if you like.

Makes 21 pieces

Cake tin needed: a 30 x 23cm (12 x 9in) traybake or roasting tin

225g (8oz) butter, softened

225g (8oz) caster sugar

275g (10oz) self-raising flour

2 level tsp baking powder

4 large eggs

4 tbsp milk

a little sifted icing sugar, for dusting (optional)

Step one Preheat the oven to 180°C/Fan 160°C/gas 4. Grease the tin then line the base with non-stick baking parchment.

Step two Measure all the ingredients except the icing sugar into a large bowl and beat until well blended. Turn the mixture into the prepared tin and level the top.

Step three Bake for 35–40 minutes or until the cake has shrunk from the sides of the tin and springs back when pressed in the centre with your fingertips. Leave to cool in the tin, then cut into pieces and peel off the non-stick baking parchment.

To make a larger traybake, grease a 29 x 36cm (11⅛ x 14⅛in) traybake or roasting tin and line the base with non-stick baking parchment. Measure 350g (12oz) softened butter, 350g (12oz) caster sugar, 450g (1lb) self-raising flour, 2 level tsp baking powder, 6 large eggs and 6 tbsp milk into a large bowl and beat until well blended. Bake for 40–45 minutes or until the cake has shrunk from the sides of the tin and springs back when pressed in the centre with your fingertips. Leave to cool in the tin before cutting into 36 pieces and peeling off the non-stick baking parchment.

Iced Chocolate Traybake

Chocolate cakes are always popular, and this is a particularly simple version, which is great for family teas or lunch boxes.

Step one Preheat the oven to 180°C/Fan 160°C/gas 4. Grease the tin then line the base with non-stick baking parchment.

Step two Blend together the cocoa and hot water then allow to cool slightly. Measure all the cake ingredients into a large bowl and beat until well blended. Turn the mixture into the prepared tin and level the surface.

Step three Bake for 35–40 minutes or until the cake has shrunk from the sides of the tin and springs back when pressed in the centre with your fingertips. Leave to cool in the tin.

Step four To make the icing, warm the apricot jam in a pan and brush all over the cake. Break the chocolate into pieces and melt in a pan with the water, heating gently until melted and smooth. Leave to cool slightly, then beat in the icing sugar and oil. Pour over the cold cake and smooth over gently with a palette knife. Leave to set for about 30 minutes, then cut into pieces and decorate with chocolate curls.

If time allows, do brush the cold cake with apricot jam before icing. It gives the cake a lovely flavour and prevents crumbs from the cake getting into the icing.

Makes 21 pieces

Cake tin needed:
a 30 x 23cm (12 x 9in) traybake or roasting tin

4 level tbsp cocoa powder

4 tbsp hot water

225g (8oz) butter, softened

225g (8oz) caster sugar

275g (10oz) self-raising flour

2 level tsp baking powder

4 large eggs

4 tbsp milk

for the icing and decoration

4 tbsp apricot jam

150g (5oz) plain chocolate (39 per cent cocoa solids)

6 tbsp water

350g (12oz) sifted icing sugar

1 tsp sunflower oil

chocolate curls (see page 52)

Chocolate Chip and Vanilla Marble Cake

This is a popular traybake for parties, and children particularly enjoy the fun of making marble cakes.

Makes 21 small pieces

Cake tin needed: a 30 x 23cm (12 x 9in) traybake or roasting tin

225g (8oz) butter, softened

225g (8oz) caster sugar

275g (10oz) self-raising flour

2 level tsp baking powder

4 large eggs

2 tbsp milk

½ tsp vanilla extract

1½ level tbsp cocoa powder

2 tbsp hot water

50g (2oz) plain chocolate chips

for the icing

50g (2oz) plain chocolate (39 per cent cocoa solids)

50g (2oz) Belgian white chocolate

Step one Preheat the oven to 180°C/Fan 160°C/gas 4. Grease the tin and line the base with non-stick baking parchment.

Step two Measure the butter, sugar, flour, baking powder, eggs, milk and vanilla extract into a large bowl and beat well for about 2 minutes until well blended. Spoon half the mixture into the prepared tin, dotting the spoonfuls apart.

Step three In a small bowl, blend the cocoa and hot water. Cool slightly, then add it to the remaining cake mixture along with the chocolate chips. Spoon this chocolate mixture in between the plain cake mixture to fill the gaps.

Step four Bake for 35–40 minutes or until the cake has shrunk from the sides of the tin and springs back when pressed in the centre with your fingertips. Leave to cool in the tin.

Step five To make the icing, break the plain and white chocolate into pieces and melt them separately. Spoon into two separate small plastic bags, snip off a corner of each bag and drizzle the chocolates all over the top of the cake to decorate. Leave to set for about 30 minutes before cutting into squares.

Family Fruit Teabread

You need to start this teabread the day before, as the dried fruits have to be soaked in hot tea overnight to give them time to swell. If you have tea left in the pot, use that instead of making it specially. Allow the cooked cake to cool completely, then store in an airtight tin.

Step one Put the mixed dried fruit and the sugar into a bowl, stir to mix, then pour over the hot tea. Cover the bowl and leave in a cool place overnight to allow the fruit to plump up.

Step two Preheat the oven to 150°C/Fan 130°C/gas 2. Lightly grease the tin and line it with a wide strip of non-stick baking parchment to go up the wide sides and over the base.

Step three Add the flour, lemon zest and beaten egg to the fruit mixture and stir with a wooden spoon until thoroughly mixed. Turn the mixture into the prepared tin and gently level the surface.

Step four Bake for 1¼–1½ hours, until the teabread is well risen and firm to the touch and a fine skewer inserted in the centre comes out clean. Leave to cool in the tin for about 10 minutes, then loosen with a small palette knife. Turn the teabread out and leave on a wire rack to cool. Peel off the parchment and serve the teabread sliced and buttered.

Cake tin needed:
a 900g (2lb) loaf
tin, 17 x 9 x 9cm
(6½ x 3½ x 3½ in)
base measurement

350g (12oz) mixed
dried fruit

225g (8oz) light
muscovado sugar

300ml (½ pint) hot
Earl Grey tea, made
using 2 tsp Earl Grey
tea or 2 tea bags

275g (10oz) self-
raising flour

zest of 1 lemon

1 large egg, beaten

Banana Loaf

This is a lovely, moist loaf, which really doesn't need to be buttered. It freezes extremely well. Any bananas left in the fruit bowl are ideal for this cake – the riper they are, the better.

Cake tin needed:
a 900g (2lb) loaf tin, 17 x 9 x 9cm (6½ x 3½ x 3½ in) base measurement

100g (4oz) butter, softened

175g (6oz) caster sugar

2 large eggs

2 ripe bananas, mashed

225g (8oz) self-raising flour

1 level tsp baking powder

2 tbsp milk

Step one Preheat the oven to 180°C/Fan 160°C/gas 4. Lightly grease the tin and line it with non-stick baking parchment.

Step two Measure all the ingredients into a mixing bowl and beat for about 2 minutes, until well blended; an electric mixer is best for this, but of course you can also beat by hand with a wooden spoon. Spoon the mixture into the prepared tin and level the surface.

Step three Bake for about 1 hour, until well risen and golden brown. A fine skewer inserted in the centre of the cake should come out clean. Leave the cake to cool in the tin for a few minutes, then loosen with a small palette knife and turn the cake out. Peel off the parchment and leave on a wire rack to cool completely. Slice thickly to serve.

For Mary Berry's baking tips, go to
www.mykitchentable.co.uk/authors/MaryBerry/bakingtips

Classic Sticky Gingerbread

This keeps and freezes extremely well. Sometimes you get a dip in the middle of the gingerbread, which indicates that you have been a bit heavy-handed with the syrup and treacle. It just means it tastes even more moreish.

Step one Preheat the oven to 160°C/Fan 140°C/gas 3. Cut a rectangle of non-stick baking parchment to fit the base and sides of the tin. Lightly grease the tin and then line it with the paper, pushing it neatly into the corners.

Step two Measure the butter, sugar, golden syrup and black treacle into a medium pan and heat gently until the mixture has melted evenly, stirring occasionally. Allow to cool slightly.

Step three Put the flours and ground ginger into a large mixing bowl and stir together lightly. Beat the eggs into the milk. Pour the cooled butter and syrup mixture into the flour along with the egg and milk mixture and beat with a wooden spoon until smooth. Pour the mixture into the prepared tin and tilt gently to level the surface.

Step four Bake for about 50 minutes, until well risen, golden and springy to the touch. Allow the gingerbread to cool a little in the tin, then turn out onto a wire rack and leave to cool completely. Cut into squares.

Makes 16 generous pieces

Cake tin needed:
a 30 x 23 x 4cm
(12 x 9 x 1½ in)
traybake or roasting
tin

225g (8oz) butter

225g (8oz) light
muscovado sugar

225g (8oz) golden
syrup

225g (8oz) black
treacle

225g (8oz) self-raising
flour

225g (8oz) wholemeal
self-raising flour

4 level tsp ground
ginger

2 large eggs

300ml (½ pint) milk

Coffee Fudge Squares

Walnuts and coffee make a wonderful pairing and their bitterness contrasts the sweetness of the butter icing beautifully.

Makes 21 squares

Cake tin needed:
a 30 x 23cm (12 x 9in) traybake or roasting tin

175g (6oz) butter, softened

175g (6oz) caster sugar

225g (8oz) self-raising flour

1½ level tsp baking powder

3 large eggs

2 tbsp milk

1 tbsp coffee essence

for the fudge topping

50g (2oz) butter

115g (4oz) light muscovado sugar

2 tbsp milk

280g (10oz) icing sugar, sifted

25g (1oz) chopped walnuts

Step one Preheat the oven to 180°C/Fan 160°C/gas 4. Grease the tin and then line the base with greased non-stick baking parchment. Alternatively, you could line the tin with greased foil.

Step two Place all the cake ingredients in a large bowl and beat well for 2 minutes or until well blended. Transfer to the tin and level the top.

Step three Bake for 30–35 minutes or until the cake has shrunk from the sides of the tin and springs back when pressed in the centre with your fingertips. Leave to cool in the tin.

Step four To make the fudge topping; place the butter, sugar and milk in a small pan and heat gently until the sugar dissolves, stirring occasionally, then boil briskly for 3 minutes. Remove from the heat and gradually stir in the icing sugar. Beat thoroughly until smooth. Spread quickly over the top of the cake and sprinkle over the walnuts. Leave to set, then cut the cake into squares and lift out using a palette knife.

While it is best to use coffee essence in terms of flavour and colour, you can substitute two teaspoons of instant coffee dissolved in one tablespoon of hot water for each tablespoon of coffee essence.

Courgette Loaves

Expect this cake to have a sugary top, which is quite normal. This recipe makes two loaves – freeze one and store the other in the fridge. Serve sliced and buttered, or spread with low-fat soft cheese.

Step one Preheat the oven to 180°C/Fan 160°C/gas 4. Grease the tin then line the bases with non-stick baking parchment.

Step two Measure all the ingredients into a large bowl and mix well to make a thick batter. Pour into the prepared tins.

Step three Bake for about 1 hour or until the loaves are firm and a skewer inserted into the centre comes out clean. Leave to cool in the tins for 10 minutes then turn out, peel off the parchment and finish cooling on a wire rack. Store in the fridge and use within 3 weeks.

Cake tins needed:
2 x 900g (2lb) loaf tins

3 large eggs

250ml (9½ fl oz) sunflower oil

350g (12oz) caster sugar

350g (12oz) courgettes (or small marrow), grated

165g (5½ oz) plain flour

165g (5½ oz) buckwheat flour

1 level tsp baking powder

2 level tsp bicarbonate of soda

1 level tbsp ground cinnamon

175g (6oz) raisins

150g (5oz) chopped walnuts

Bath Buns

The spa town of Bath is famous for its buns, distinguished by the coarse sugar topping. They are said to have been created in the eighteenth century.

Makes about 18 buns

Cake tins needed:
2 baking sheets

450g (1lb) strong white flour

7g sachet fast-action yeast

1 level tsp salt

50g (2oz) caster sugar

50g (2oz) butter, melted and cooled

2 large eggs, beaten

150ml (¼ pint) tepid milk

175g (6oz) sultanas

50g (2oz) chopped candied peel

to finish

1 large egg, to glaze

nibbed sugar or coarsely crushed sugar cubes

Step one Lightly grease the baking sheets.

Step two Measure the flour, yeast, salt and caster sugar into a large bowl and mix well. Make a well in the centre and pour in the melted, cooled butter, eggs and milk, adding the sultanas and chopped peel last. Mix to a smooth, soft dough.

Step three Turn the dough out onto a lightly floured work surface and knead for about 5 minutes or until smooth and elastic. Place in an oiled bowl and cover with oiled clingfilm, or put the bowl inside a large polythene bag. Leave to rise until doubled in size, about 1 hour in a warm room.

Step four Turn the risen dough out of the bowl and knead well until the dough is again smooth and elastic. Divide into 18 equal pieces. Shape each piece of dough into a bun and place on the prepared baking sheets. Cover again with oiled clingfilm and leave in a warm place until doubled in size, about 30 minutes. Preheat the oven to 190°C/Fan 170°C/gas 5.

Step five Brush the buns with beaten egg and sprinkle with nibbed sugar. Bake for about 15 minutes or until golden brown and the buns sound hollow when the base is tapped. Lift onto a wire rack to cool. Serve buttered.

Devonshire Scones

The secret to good scones is not to handle them too much before baking, and to make the mixture on the wet, sticky side.

Step one Preheat the oven to 220°C/Fan 200°C/gas 7. Lightly grease the baking sheets.

Step two Put the flour and baking powder into a large bowl. Add the butter and rub it in with your fingertips until the mixture resembles fine breadcrumbs. Stir in the sugar. Beat the eggs together and make up to a generous 300ml (½ pint) with the milk, then put about two tablespoons of the mixture aside in a cup for glazing the scones later. Gradually add the egg mixture to the dry ingredients, stirring it in until you have a soft dough. It is far better that the scone mixture is on the wet side, sticking to your fingers, as the scones will rise better.

Step three Turn the dough out onto a lightly floured surface and flatten it with your hand or a rolling pin to a thickness of 1–2cm (½–1in). Use a 5cm (2in) fluted cutter to stamp out the scones by pushing the cutter straight down into the dough (as opposed to twisting it), then lifting it straight out. This ensures that the scones will rise evenly and keep their shape. Gently push the remaining dough together, knead very lightly then re-roll and cut out more scones in the same way.

Step four Arrange the scones on the prepared baking sheets and brush the tops with the reserved beaten egg mixture to glaze. Bake for 10–15 minutes, until well risen and golden, then transfer to a wire rack and leave to cool, covered with a clean tea towel to keep them moist. Serve as fresh as possible, cut in half and spread generously with strawberry jam. Top with a good spoonful of thick cream as well, if you like.

Either eat the scones on the day of making or leave them to cool completely and then freeze. If time allows, thaw them at room temperature for a couple of hours and then refresh in a moderate oven for about 10 minutes.

Makes 8–10 large (9cm/3½ in) scones or 20 smaller ones

Cake tins needed:
2 baking sheets

450g (1lb) self-raising flour

2 rounded tsp baking powder

75g (3oz) butter, at room temperature

50g (2oz) caster sugar

2 large eggs

about 225ml (8fl oz) milk

to serve

raspberry jam

clotted cream or pouring double cream, whipped

Special Fruit Scones

Making good scones is so easy if the mixture is not too dry and the dough is not overhandled. Wrap the scones in a clean tea towel after baking to keep them moist.

Makes about 14 scones

Cake tins needed:
2 baking sheets

225g (8oz) self-raising flour

1 level tsp baking powder

50g (2oz) butter, softened

25g (1oz) caster sugar

50g (2oz) mixed dried fruit

1 large egg

a little milk

Step one Preheat the oven to 220°C/Fan 200°C/gas 7. Lightly grease the baking sheets.

Step two Measure the flour and baking powder into a large bowl, add the butter and rub in with your fingertips until the mixture resembles fine breadcrumbs. Stir in the sugar and the dried fruit. Break the egg into a measuring jug and beat, then make up to 150ml (¼ pint) with milk. Stir the egg and milk into the flour and mix to a soft but not sticky dough.

Step three Turn out onto a lightly floured work surface, knead lightly and roll out to a 1cm (½in) thickness. Cut into rounds with a fluted 5cm (2in) cutter and place them on the prepared baking sheets. Brush the tops with a little milk.

Step four Bake for about 10 minutes or until pale golden brown. Lift the scones onto a wire rack to cool. Eat as fresh as possible.

Orange Scotch Pancakes

In the old days, these were made on a solid metal griddle over an open fire. Now it is more practical to use a large, non-stick frying pan.

Step one Grate the zest from the oranges and set aside, and then squeeze the juice. Pour the juice into a measuring jug and make it up to 200ml (7fl oz) with milk.

Step two Measure the flour, baking powder, sugar and orange zest into a mixing bowl. Make a well in the centre and add the egg and half the orange juice and milk mixture. Beat well to make a smooth, thick batter and then beat in enough of the remaining orange juice and milk to give a batter the consistency of thick cream.

Step three Heat a large, non-stick frying pan over a medium heat and grease with a little oil or white vegetable fat. Drop the mixture in dessertspoonfuls onto the hot pan, spacing them well apart to allow the mixture to spread. When bubbles appear on the surface, turn the pancakes over with a blunt-endod non-stick palette knife or a spatula and cook on the other side for 30 seconds–1 minute, until golden brown. Transfer to a wire rack and cover with a clean tea towel to keep them soft. Cook the remaining mixture in the same way. Serve immediately, with butter and golden or maple syrup, and orange zest, if liked.

Makes about 24 pancakes

Cookware needed:
a frying pan

2 oranges, plus a little zest for sprinkling (optional)

a little milk

175g (6oz) self-raising flour

1 level tsp baking powder

40g (1½oz) caster sugar

1 large egg

a little oil or white vegetable fat, for greasing

butter and golden syrup or maple syrup, to serve

Drop Scones

These are also known as Scotch pancakes. If you make them in advance and need to reheat them, arrange them in a single layer on an ovenproof dish, cover tightly with foil and reheat in a moderate oven for about 10 minutes.

Makes about 21 pancakes

Cookware needed: a griddle or frying pan

175g (6oz) self-raising flour

1 level tsp baking powder

40g (1½ oz) caster sugar

1 large egg

about 200ml (7fl oz) milk

Butter and golden syrup, to serve

Step one Prepare either a griddle or a heavy-based frying pan (preferably non-stick) by heating and greasing with oil or white vegetable fat.

Step two Measure the flour, baking powder and sugar into a large bowl, make a well in the centre and then add the egg and half the milk. Beat to a smooth, thick batter, then beat in enough of the remaining milk to give the batter the consistency of thick cream.

Step three Drop the mixture in tablespoonfuls onto the hot griddle or frying pan, spacing the mixture well apart. When bubbles rise to the surface, turn the scones over with a palette knife and cook on the other side for a further 30 seconds– 1 minute, until golden brown. Lift off onto a wire rack and cover them with a clean tea towel to keep them soft. Cook the remaining mixture in the same way. Serve warm, with butter and golden syrup.

Singin' Hinny

This Northumberland griddle cake 'sings' or sizzles as it cooks on the griddle, hence its name. 'Hinny' is Northern slang for honey, a term of endearment applied especially to children and young women. Traditionally the Singin' Hinny is made in one large round, but you can make two or three smaller ones in the same way.

Step one Prepare a griddle or large heavy-based frying pan (preferably non-stick) by heating and lightly greasing it with oil or white vegetable fat.

Step two Measure the flour, bicarbonate of soda and cream of tartar into a large bowl, add the lard or white vegetable fat and rub in with your fingertips until the mixture resembles fine breadcrumbs. Stir in the currants. Mix to a soft but not sticky dough with the milk and turn out onto a lightly floured work surface. Knead lightly then roll out to a large round about 5mm (¼in) thick.

Step three Lift the scone round onto the prepared hot griddle and cook on a gentle heat for about 5 minutes on one side, then carefully turn over and cook on the other side for a further 5 minutes or until both sides are a good brown. Slide the Singin' Hinny onto a wire rack to cool slightly, then split and butter, sandwich back together and serve hot.

Serves 4–6

Cookware needed:
a griddle or frying pan

350g (12oz) plain flour

½ level tsp bicarbonate of soda

1 level tsp cream of tartar

75g (3oz) lard or white vegetable fat (not butter)

100g (4oz) currants

about 200ml (7fl oz) milk

Griddle Scones

Make these with either white or wholemeal flour and eat them really fresh, spread with butter. If you use wholemeal flour, the mixture will need a little more milk.

Makes about 12 scones

Cookware needed: a griddle or frying pan

225g (8oz) plain or wholemeal flour

1 level tsp bicarbonate of soda

2 level tsp cream of tartar

25g (1oz) butter

25g (1oz) caster sugar

about 150ml (¼ pint) milk

Step one Prepare a griddle or heavy-based frying pan by heating and lightly greasing with oil or white vegetable fat.

Step two Measure the flour, bicarbonate of soda and cream of tartar into a large bowl, add the butter and rub in with your fingertips until the mixture resembles fine breadcrumbs. Stir in the sugar and gradually add the milk, mixing the dough with a round-bladed knife to a soft but not sticky dough.

Step three Divide the dough in half and knead each piece very lightly on a lightly floured work surface. Roll out each piece into a round about 1cm (½ in) thick, then cut each round into six equal wedges. Cook the wedges in batches on the prepared hot griddle for about 5 minutes each side until evenly brown. Lift onto a wire rack to cool. Eat as fresh as possible.

It is traditional to use bicarbonate of soda and cream of tartar, but you can use self-raising flour and 2 tsp of baking powder instead.

Welsh Cakes

For sweet cakes it is traditional to use a fluted cutter, but you may find a plain cutter easier for these as it will cut through the fruit in the dough more easily.

Step one Prepare a griddle or heavy-based frying pan by heating and lightly greasing with oil.

Step two Measure the flour and baking powder into a large bowl and rub in the butter with your fingertips until the mixture resembles fine breadcrumbs. Add the sugar, currants and spice.

Step three Beat the egg and milk together, then add this to the mixture and mix to form a firm dough, adding a little more milk if necessary. Roll out the dough onto a lightly floured work surface to a thickness of 5mm (¼in) then cut into rounds with a 7.5cm (3in) plain round cutter.

Step four Cook the dough rounds on the hot griddle on a low heat for about 3 minutes on each side until golden brown (be careful not to cook them too fast, otherwise the centres will not be fully cooked). Cool on a wire rack then sprinkle with caster sugar. They should be eaten on the day of making, served buttered.

Makes about 18 cakes

Cookware needed:
a griddle or frying pan

350g (12oz) self-raising flour

2 level tsp baking powder

175g (6oz) butter

115g (4½ oz) caster sugar

100g (4oz) currants

¾ level tsp ground mixed spice

1 large egg

about 2 tbsp milk

caster sugar, for sprinkling

Hot Cross Buns

This used to be baked as one large bun, but now it is usual to have individual buns.

Makes about 12 buns

Cake tins needed:
2 baking sheets

450g (1lb) strong white flour

1 level tsp salt

1 level tsp ground mixed spice

1 level tsp ground cinnamon

½ level tsp freshly grated nutmeg

7g sachet fast-action yeast

50g (2oz) caster sugar

50g (2oz) butter, melted and cooled

150ml (¼ pint) tepid milk

5 tbsp tepid water

1 large egg, beaten

75g (3oz) currants

50g (2oz) chopped candied peel

for the glazing

2 tbsp granulated sugar

2 tbsp water

Step one Lightly grease the baking sheets.

Step two Measure the flour, salt, spices, yeast and sugar into a large bowl and stir to mix. Make a well in the centre and pour in the melted, cooled butter, milk, water and egg, then add the currants and chopped peel.

Step three Mix to a soft dough, then turn out onto a lightly floured work surface and knead for about 10 minutes until smooth and elastic. Transfer to an oiled bowl, cover with oiled clingfilm and leave to rise until the dough has doubled in size, about 1½ hours in a warm room. (Because this is an enriched dough, it will take longer to rise than a plain dough.)

Step four Turn the risen dough out onto a lightly floured work surface again and knead for 2–3 minutes. Divide the dough into 12 equal pieces and shape each one into a round bun. Make a cross in the top of each bun with a knife, then place onto the prepared baking sheets and cover with oiled clingfilm. Leave to rise again in a warm place until doubled in size, about 30 minutes. Preheat the oven to 220°C/Fan 200°C/gas 7.

Step five Bake the buns for about 15 minutes until brown and hollow-sounding when the base is tapped. While the buns are baking, make the glazing by dissolving the sugar in the water over a gentle heat. As soon as the buns come out of the oven, brush them with the syrup to give a sticky glaze.

For a more definite cross on the top of the buns, make up 50g (2oz) of shortcrust pastry (using 50g/2oz plain flour and 25g/1oz butter and a little water), cut it into thin strips and lay it over the top of the buns before baking.

Sultana Streusel Buns

These are fairly plain buns that are best eaten freshly baked. If you want to make slightly smaller buns but don't have two bun tins, cook them in two batches – the recipe can stretch to 18 buns.

Step one Preheat the oven to 190°C/Fan 170°C/gas 5. Place fairy cake cases in the bun tin.

Step two Measure the flour and baking powder into a large bowl. Add the butter and rub in with your fingertips until the mixture resembles fine breadcrumbs. Stir in the sugar and sultanas.

Step three Lightly mix the egg and milk together and add all at once to the dry mixture. Beat well to give a smooth mixture, then spoon into the paper cases.

Step four To make the streusel topping, mix together the flour and sugar and add the melted butter. Use a fork to mix until crumbly. Sprinkle this mixture over the tops of the buns.

Step five Bake for about 15 minutes until well risen and firm to the touch. Lift the paper cake cases out of the bun tin and leave to cool on a wire rack. If you are making 18 buns, add six more fairy cake cases to the tin and bake. Dust the buns with icing sugar to serve.

Makes 12–18 buns

Cake tin needed:
a 12-hole bun tin

225g (8oz) self-raising flour

1 level tsp baking powder

75g (3oz) butter

75g (3oz) caster sugar

50g (2oz) sultanas

1 large egg

150ml (¼ pint) milk

for the streusel topping

25g (1oz) self-raising flour

50g (2oz) light muscovado sugar

25g (1oz) butter, melted

icing sugar, for dusting

Cheese and Olive Scone Bake

Making one large scone is fastest of all, as you don't have to roll and cut out the mixture. If you don't have a traybake or roasting tin, shape the dough into an oblong on a baking sheet.

Makes 12 squares

Cake tin needed:
a 30 x 23cm (12 x 9in)
traybake or roasting
tin

450g (1lb) self-raising
flour

2 level tsp baking
powder

1 level tsp salt

100g (4oz) butter

200g (7oz) mature
Cheddar, grated

100g (4oz) pitted
black olives, roughly
chopped

2 large eggs

a little milk

25g (1oz) grated
Parmesan

Step one Preheat the oven to 230°C/Fan 210°C/gas 8. Lightly grease the tin.

Step two Measure the flour, baking powder and salt into a large bowl. Add the butter and rub in with your fingertips until the mixture resembles fine breadcrumbs. Stir in the grated Cheddar and the roughly chopped olives. Break the eggs into a measuring jug and make up to 300ml (½ pint) with milk. Add to the flour mixture, mixing to form a soft dough.

Step three Knead the dough quickly and lightly until smooth, then roll out onto a lightly floured work surface to an oblong to fit the tin. Transfer to the prepared tin and mark into 12 squares, then brush the top with a little milk.

Step four Bake for about 15 minutes. Sprinkle the top with the Parmesan and bake for a further 5 minutes or until the scone is well risen and golden. Turn out onto a wire rack to cool.

Potato Scones

These scones are particularly moist, excellent if you want to keep them a day or two. They can be made sweet or savoury.

Step one Preheat the oven to 220°C/Fan 200°C/gas 7. Lightly grease the baking sheets.

Step two Measure the flour and baking powder into a large bowl, add the butter and rub in with your fingertips until the mixture resembles fine breadcrumbs. Stir in the sugar and the mashed potato, mixing with a fork to prevent the potato from forming lumps. Add enough milk to form a soft but not sticky dough.

Step three Turn the mixture out onto a lightly floured work surface and knead very lightly. Roll out to a thickness of about 1cm (½in) and cut into rounds using a 5cm (2in) fluted cutter (use a plain cutter for savoury scones). Transfer to the baking sheets

Step four Bake for about 12 minutes or until well risen and golden brown. Serve warm and buttered.

For savoury Potato Scones, omit the sugar and add half a teaspoon of salt to the flour.

Makes about 12 scones

Cake tins needed:
2 baking sheets

175g (6oz) plain flour

3 level tsp baking powder

50g (2oz) butter

40g (1½oz) caster sugar

100g (4oz) fresh mashed potato

about 3 tbsp milk

Cheese Scone Round

Serve these scone wedges warm with cold meats, soup or a cheese board – and with butter, of course!

Makes 1 large scone round marked into 6 wedges

Cake tin needed:
a baking sheet

225g (8oz) self-raising flour

½ level tsp salt

½ level tsp mustard powder

¼ level tsp cayenne pepper

1 level tsp baking powder

25g (1oz) butter

150g (5oz) grated mature Cheddar

1 large egg

a little milk

Step one Preheat the oven to 220°C/Fan 200°C/gas 7. Lightly grease the baking sheet.

Step two Measure the flour, salt, mustard powder, cayenne pepper and baking powder into a large bowl. Add the butter and rub in with your fingertips until the mixture resembles fine breadcrumbs. Stir in 100g (4oz) of the grated cheese.

Step three Break the egg into a measuring jug then make up to 150ml (¼ pint) with milk. Stir the egg and milk into the dry ingredients and mix to a soft but not sticky dough.

Step four Turn out onto a lightly floured work surface and knead lightly. Roll out to a 15cm (6in) circle. Transfer to the prepared baking sheet and mark into six wedges. Brush with a little milk and sprinkle with the remaining grated cheese.

Step five Bake for about 15 minutes or until golden brown and firm to the touch. Slide onto a wire rack to cool. Eat as fresh as possible.

Chocolate and Vanilla Marble Loaf

This loaf cake looks spectacular and is lovely for a special occasion. It easily slices into ten.

Step one Preheat the oven to 160°C/Fan 140°C/gas 3. Lightly grease the tin and line with a wide strip of non-stick baking parchment to go up the wide sides and over the base of the tin.

Step two Measure the butter, sugar, flour, baking powder, eggs, milk and vanilla extract into a large bowl and beat with a hand-held electric mixer for about 2 minutes, until well blended. Spoon half the mixture into another bowl and set aside.

Step three In a small bowl, mix the cocoa powder and hot water together until smooth. Allow to cool slightly, then add to one of the bowls of cake mixture, mixing well until evenly blended.

Step four Spoon the vanilla and chocolate cake mixtures randomly into the prepared tin until all of the mixture is used up, and gently level the surface. Bake for 50 minutes–1 hour, until the cake is well risen, springy to the touch and beginning to shrink away from the sides of the tin. Allow to cool in the tin for a few minutes, then turn out onto a wire rack, peel off the lining paper and leave to cool completely.

Step five To make the icing, melt the butter in a small pan, add the cocoa powder, stir to blend and cook gently for 1 minute. Stir in the milk and icing sugar, then remove from the heat and mix thoroughly. If necessary, leave the icing on one side, stirring occasionally, to thicken. Spread the cold cake evenly with the icing, then drizzle the melted white chocolate over the top. Leave to set.

Serves 10

Cake tin needed:
a 900g (2lb) loaf tin, 17 x 9 x 9cm (6½ x 3½ x 3½in) base measurement

225g (8oz) butter, softened

225g (8oz) caster sugar

275g (10oz) self-raising flour

2 level tsp baking powder

4 large eggs

2 tbsp milk

¼ tsp vanilla extract

1½ level tbsp cocoa powder

2 tbsp hot water

for the icing

25g (1oz) butter

15g (½ oz) cocoa powder, sifted

1–2 tbsp milk

100g (4oz) icing sugar, sifted

about 25g (1oz) white chocolate, melted

For step-by-step photographs of this recipe, go to
www.mykitchentable.co.uk/recipes/chocolatevanillaloaf

English Madeleines

For this recipe, you will need dariole moulds, which are available from specialist cook shops and department stores. If you don't have ten, make the madeleines in batches.

Makes 10 cakes

Cake tins needed: 10 dariole moulds

100g (4oz) butter, softened

100g (4oz) caster sugar

2 large eggs

100g (4oz) self-raising flour

1 level tsp baking powder

2–3 drops vanilla extract

to finish

4 tbsp raspberry or strawberry jam

50g (2oz) desiccated coconut

5 red or natural glacé cherries

Step one Preheat the oven to 180°C/Fan 160°C/gas 4. Grease the moulds then line the base of each with non-stick baking parchment. Stand the moulds on a baking sheet.

Step two Measure the cake ingredients into a large bowl and beat until the mixture is well blended and smooth. Spoon the mixture into the moulds, filling them about half full.

Step three Bake for about 20 minutes until well risen and firm to the touch. Leave to cool in the moulds for 5 minutes then turn out, peel off the parchment and finish cooling on a wire rack.

Step four When the cakes are cool, trim the bases so that they stand firmly. Push the raspberry or strawberry jam through a sieve, then put into a small pan and warm through. Spread the coconut out on a large plate. Use a fork to spear the bases of the cakes to hold them. Brush them with the warm jam, then roll in the coconut to coat. Cut the glacé cherries in half and decorate each madeleine with a half.

French Madeleines

These shell-shaped cakes are made using a madeleine tin, available from specialist kitchen shops. Madeleines are best eaten on the day of making and, in France, are traditionally dipped into tea to eat.

Step one Preheat the oven to 220°C/Fan 200°C/gas 7. Grease a madeleine tray, dust with flour and shake off any excess – the cakes will then come out cleanly.

Step two Melt the butter in a small pan and then allow to cool slightly. Measure the eggs and sugar into a large bowl and whisk until pale and thick.

Step three Sift in half the flour along with the baking powder and the lemon zest and fold in gently. Pour in half the melted butter around the edge of the bowl and fold in. Repeat the process with the remaining flour and butter. Spoon the mixture into the prepared tray so that the mixture is just level in the moulds.

Step four Bake for 8–10 minutes or until well risen, golden and springy to the touch. Ease out of the tray with a small palette knife and cool on a wire rack. Grease and flour the tray again and repeat until all the mixture has been used up.

Makes 30 cakes

Cake tin needed: a madeleine tray – bake in batches if you haven't enough

150g (5oz) butter

3 large eggs

150g (5oz) caster sugar

150g (5oz) self-raising flour

½ **level tsp baking powder**

zest of 1 lemon

Sachertorte

A superb rich, very densely textured chocolate cake, named after the Sacher hotel in Vienna. Ground almonds replace the flour, which means the cake keeps well.

Cake tin needed:
a deep, round, loose-based 23cm (9in) cake tin

265g (9½ oz) plain chocolate (39 per cent cocoa solids), broken into pieces

6 large eggs, 5 of them separated

215g (7½ oz) caster sugar

150g (5oz) ground almonds

for the topping and icing

about 4 tbsp apricot jam

150g (5oz) plain chocolate (39 per cent cocoa solids), broken into pieces

150ml (¼ pint) pouring double cream

25g (1oz) white chocolate

Step one Preheat the oven to 180°C/Fan 160°C/gas 4. Grease the cake tin and line the base with non-stick baking parchment.

Step two Put the chocolate into a bowl placed over a pan of hot water. Place the pan over a low heat until the chocolate has melted, stirring occasionally. Allow to cool a little.

Step three Whisk the 5 egg whites in a large mixing bowl until stiff but not dry. In a separate large mixing bowl, use a hand-held electric mixer to whisk together the 5 egg yolks, whole egg and sugar until thick and pale. The mixture should be thick enough to leave a trail on the surface when the whisk is lifted from the bowl.

Step four Whisk the ground almonds, melted chocolate and 1 tbsp of the whisked egg whites into the egg yolk mixture. Carefully fold in the remaining egg whites using a large metal spoon or a straight-edged plastic spatula. Turn the mixture into the tin.

Step five Bake for 40–45 minutes, until the crust that forms on the top is firm and the cake has begun to shrink away from the side of the tin. Allow the cake to cool in the tin for about 10 minutes before loosening it around the edge with a small palette knife. Turn the cake upside down onto a wire rack covered with a tea towel. Peel off the parchment and leave to cool completely.

Step six Gently heat the apricot jam in a smal pan and then brush it evenly over the top and sides of the cake. To make the icing, put the chocolate into a bowl with the double cream and melt slowly over a pan of hot water. Stir occasionally until smooth and glossy. Allow the icing to cool and thicken slightly, then pour it onto the centre of the cake. Spread it gently over the top and down the sides with a palette knife and leave to set. To finish, melt the white chocolate slowly in a bowl over a pan of hot water. Spoon into a small paper icing bag or polythene bag, snip off the corner and pipe 'Sacher' across the cake and leave to set.

Swiss Wild Strawberry and Walnut Cake

This is a light walnut sponge filled with wild strawberries and cream, often served on the Continent as a pudding. For a lighter filling, you can use crème fraîche, and you can use regular strawberries when wild strawberries are out of season.

Step one Preheat the oven to 180°C/Fan 160°C/gas 4. Grease the tin then line the base with non-stick baking parchment.

Step two Measure the eggs and sugar into a large bowl and beat until the mixture is thick and mousse-like and leaves a trail when the whisk is lifted out of the mixture. Sift the flour onto the mixture and lightly fold in along with the chopped walnuts. Turn into the prepared cake tin.

Step three Bake for 40–45 minutes or until well risen and the top of the cake springs back when lightly pressed with a finger. Leave to cool in the tin for a few minutes then turn out, peel off the parchment and finish cooling on a wire rack.

Step four When the cake is cold, cut it into three horizontally. Sandwich the slices together with a good amount of whipped cream and strawberries. Spread the remaining cream over the top and the sides of the cake and decorate with the reserved strawberries.

Cake tin needed:
a deep, round 20cm
(8in) cake tin

3 large eggs

100g (4oz) caster
sugar

75g (3oz) self-raising
flour

50g (2oz) roughly
chopped walnuts

**for the filling and
topping**

300ml (½ pint)
whipping or pouring
double cream,
whipped

450g (1lb) wild
strawberries, plus
extra for decorating

For a video masterclass on icing a cake, go to
www.mykitchentable.co.uk/videos/icing

Chocolate Mousse Cake

You could use a chocolate whisked sponge for this cake, but a Genoese cake is moister and keeps better. Be very light-handed when folding in the flour and butter, or the butter will sink, resulting in a heavy cake.

Cake tin needed:
a deep, round 23cm (9in) loose-based cake tin

25g (1oz) butter

6 extra large eggs

175g (6oz) caster sugar

100g (4oz) self-raising flour

25g (1oz) cocoa powder

2 level tbsp cornflour

for the mousse filling

175g (6oz) plain chocolate (39 per cent cocoa solids), broken into pieces

2 tbsp brandy

1 level tsp powdered gelatine

2 large eggs, separated

300ml (10floz) pouring double cream

for the decoration

200g (7oz) plain chocolate (39 per cent cocoa solids), broken into pieces

150g (5oz) white chocolate, broken into pieces

150ml (5fl oz) pouring double cream, whipped

Step one Preheat the oven to 180°C/Fan 160°C/gas 4. Lightly grease the tin and line the base with greased non-stick baking parchment.

Step two Heat the butter gently in a small pan until melted. Leave to cool slightly. Whisk the eggs and sugar together until the mixture is pale and creamy and thick enough to leave a trail when the whisk is lifted from the mixture.

Step three Sift the flour, cocoa and cornflour together. Fold half the flours into the egg mixture. Pour half the cooled butter around the egg mixture and fold in. Gradually fold in the remaining flours and then the butter. Pour into the prepared tin.

Step four Bake for 35-40 minutes until well risen, firm to the touch and beginning to shrink away from the sides of the tin. Turn out onto a wire rack and leave to cool. Cut the cake in half horizontally and place the bottom half back in the clean tin.

Step five Melt the chocolate and brandy slowly in a bowl over a pan of hot water. Sprinkle the gelatine over 1 tablespoon of cold water in a bowl and leave to sponge for about 10 minutes. Stand the bowl in a pan of hot water and allow to dissolve. Stir the egg yolks into the slightly cooled melted chocolate mix. Whip the cream until it just stands in soft peaks, then fold into the chocolate. Stir in the dissolved gelatine. Whisk the egg whites until stiff and gently fold in.

Step six Pour the mousse on top of the cake in the tin, level the surface and top with the remaining cake. Cover and leave to set in the fridge. Make the chocolate curls from the chocolates (see page 52). When the mousse is set, ease around the sides of the mousse with a knife then remove the cake from the tin and place onto a serving plate. Cover with the whipped cream and sprinkle over the chocolate curls.

Black Forest Cake

This gateau, originating in Germany, was popular in the 1960s, particularly in restaurants, but home-made cakes are far superior. Don't use fresh cherries in the cake as they would discolour – but a few on top as decoration would look good.

Step one Preheat the oven to 180°C/Fan 160°C/gas 4. Lightly grease the tin and line the base with greased non-stick baking parchment.

Step two Break the eggs into a mixing bowl, add the sugar and whisk until the mixture is pale and thick enough to leave a trail when the whisk is lifted out of the bowl. Carefully fold in the sifted flour and cocoa. Turn the mixture into the prepared tin.

Step three Bake for 40–45 minutes or until the sponge is well risen and beginning to shrink away from the sides of the tin. Turn out onto a wire rack to cool and peel off the parchment.

Step four Drain the tins of cherries, reserving the juice. Reserve a few whole cherries for the top and stone the remainder. Place the cornflour in a small saucepan and slowly stir in the cherry juice. Bring slowly to the boil, stirring until thickened, then simmer for 2 minutes. Remove from the heat and cool. Add the kirsch and the stoned cherries to the sauce.

Step five Cut the sponge into three layers with a long sharp knife. Sandwich the layers together with three-quarters of the whipped cream and all of the cherry mixture. Spread a little of the remaining whipped cream around the sides of the cake and cover with the toasted flaked almonds. Pipe rosettes of cream around the top of the cake and decorate with chocolate curls and fresh cherries, if available.

Cake tin needed:
a deep, round 23cm (9in) cake tin

4 large eggs

100g (4oz) caster sugar

75g (3oz) self-raising flour, sifted

25g (1oz) cocoa powder, sifted

for the filling and topping

2 x 420g (15oz) tins black cherries

2 level tbsp cornflour

3-4 tbsp kirsch

600ml (1 pint) pouring double cream, whipped

about 50g (2oz) flaked almonds, toasted

plain chocolate curls, to decorate (see page 52)

Apple and Almond Dessert Cake

Serve this cake warm with cream either at afternoon tea or as a comforting dessert.

Cake tin needed:
a loose-based 20cm (8in) cake tin

2 large eggs

225g (8oz) caster sugar

225g (8oz) self-raising flour

1½ level tsp baking powder

½ tsp almond extract

140g (5oz) butter, melted and cooled

315g (11oz) cooking apples, peeled, cored and cut into fairly thick chunks

25g (1oz) flaked almonds

cream, to serve

Step one Preheat the oven to 160°C/Fan 140°C/gas 3. Grease the tin well.

Step two Measure the eggs, sugar, flour, baking powder, almond extract and melted butter into a large bowl. Beat together until evenly mixed. (The mixture will be like a thick sugary batter.)

Step three Spread half this mixture over the base of the tin, then top with the apple chunks. (Avoid letting the apples touch the sides of the tin.) Spoon the remaining mixture in dollops over the apples, then sprinkle with the almonds.

Step four Bake for 1½ hours or until pale golden and shrinking away from the sides of the tin. Cover lightly with foil if browning too quickly. Cool in the tin for 15 minutes, then turn out.

Devil's Food Cake

Proper American frosting requires the use of a sugar thermometer. Use the 'instant' recipe (see below) if you don't have a sugar thermometer, or simply for speed.

Step one Preheat the oven to 180°C/Fan 160°C/gas 4. Lightly grease the tins and line the bases with greased non-stick baking parchment.

Step two Whisk the cocoa into 225ml (8fl oz) water until smooth, and set aside. Place the butter in a bowl, gradually whisk in the sugar until the mixture is pale and fluffy, then gradually whisk in the eggs until evenly blended.

Step three Sift the flour, baking powder and bicarbonate of soda together and fold into the creamed mixture alternately with the cocoa and water. Divide between the tins.

Step four Bake for 30–45 minutes or until well risen and firm to the touch. Allow to cool in the tins for a few minutes, then turn out, peel off the parchment, and leave to cool completely on a wire rack.

Step five To make the American frosting, place the sugar in a large heavy-based pan with 135ml (4½fl oz) water and heat gently until the sugar has dissolved. Bring to the boil and boil until it registers 115°C/240°F on a sugar thermometer.

Step six Whisk the egg whites in a large, deep heatproof bowl until stiff. Allow the syrup bubbles to settle, then slowly pour the hot syrup onto the egg whites, whisking constantly. When all the syrup has been added, continue whisking until the mixture stands in peaks and just starts to look matt around the edges.

Step seven Sandwich the cakes together with a little frosting. Spread the remainder over the top and sides using a palette knife. Work quickly as the icing sets rapidly. Leave to set in a cool place.

To make an 'instant' American frosting, place 175g (6oz) caster sugar, one egg white, two tablespoons of hot water and a pinch of cream of tartar in a heatproof bowl over a pan of simmering water. Whisk for 10–12 minutes until thick. Use immediately.

Cake tins needed:
2 x 20cm (8in) sandwich tins

55g (2oz) cocoa powder

115g (4oz) soft butter

280g (10oz) caster sugar

2 large eggs, lightly beaten

175g (6oz) plain flour

¼ level tsp baking powder

1 level tsp bicarbonate of soda

for the American frosting
450g (1lb) caster sugar

2 large egg whites

Strawberry Pavlova

A top favourite with all ages. Traditionally the inside of the meringue is soft and marshmallow-like and the outside is crisp. Don't worry if the Pavlova cracks on the top – this is all part of its charm.

Cake tin needed:
a baking sheet

4 large egg whites

225g (8oz) caster sugar

2 level tsp cornflour

2 tsp white wine vinegar

for the filling

300ml (½ pint) whipping or pouring double cream, whipped

about 350g (12oz) strawberries, halved or sliced

Step one Preheat the oven to 160°C/Fan 140°C/gas 3. Lay a sheet of non-stick baking parchment on the baking sheet and mark a 23cm (9in) circle on it.

Step two Put the egg whites into a large bowl and whisk until stiff and cloud-like. Add the sugar a teaspoonful at a time, whisking well after each addition, until all the sugar has been added. Blend the cornflour and vinegar together and whisk into the meringue mixture. Spread the meringue out to cover the circle on the non-stick baking parchment, building up the sides so they are higher than the middle.

Step three Place in the oven but immediately reduce the temperature to 150°C/300°F/gas 2. Bake for about 1 hour until firm to the touch and a pale beige colour. Turn the oven off and allow the Pavlova to become quite cold while still in the oven. If you keep the oven door closed you will encourage a more marshmallowy meringue.

Step four Remove the cold Pavlova from the baking sheet and parchment and slide onto a serving plate. Top with the whipped cream and strawberries, then chill in the fridge for 1 hour before serving.

Mississippi Mud Pie

The origin of this pie is rather uncertain but it has become a very popular dessert in cafés and bistros. Like many American recipes, it is rich, so serve small slices.

Step one Preheat the oven to 180°C/Fan 160°C/gas 4. Grease the tin.

Step two To make the base, mix together the crushed digestive biscuits, the melted butter and the sugar and spoon into the prepared tin. Press the biscuit mixture out in an even layer, using the back of a metal spoon.

Step three To make the filling, break the chocolate into pieces and gently heat in a large pan along with the butter, instant coffee powder and water until the butter and chocolate have melted, stirring occasionally. Remove from the heat and beat in the cream, sugar and eggs. Pour the mixture onto the biscuit crust.

Step four Bake for about 1¼ hours or until set. Leave to cool completely in the tin, then turn out and decorate the top with whipped cream.

Cake tin needed:
a deep, loose-based 20cm (8in) cake tin or springform tin

for the crumb crust base

100g (4oz) crushed digestive biscuits

50g (2oz) butter, melted

25g (1oz) demerara sugar

for the filling

200g (7oz) plain chocolate (39 per cent cocoa solids)

100g (4oz) butter

1 level tbsp instant coffee powder

1 tbsp boiling water

300ml (½ pint) single cream

175g (6oz) dark muscovado sugar

6 large eggs, beaten

to finish

150ml (¼ pint) whipping or pouring double cream, whipped

Nüsskuchen

The German coffee cake comes in many forms, but always contains hazelnuts. This one is filled with a delicious apple mixture and topped with melted chocolate.

Cake tin needed:
a deep, round 20cm (8in) cake tin

40g (1½oz) shelled hazelnuts

100g (4oz) butter, softened

100g (4oz) caster sugar

2 large eggs, separated

1 level tsp instant coffee powder

1 tbsp warm milk

100g (4oz) self-raising flour

for the filling

450g (1lb) dessert apples

2 tbsp apricot jam

zest and juice of ½ lemon

to finish

50g (2oz) plain chocolate (39 per cent cocoa solids)

Step one Preheat the oven to 190°C/Fan 170°C/gas 5. Grease the tin then line the base with non-stick baking parchment.

Step two To prepare the hazelnuts, place them on a baking sheet and put into the oven for about 10 minutes. Tip onto a clean tea towel and rub the nuts together to remove the skins. (Some stubborn ones may need to go back into the oven but don't worry about getting every last bit of skin off, it's not necessary.) Place the nuts into a food processor and grind.

Step three Measure the softened butter and the sugar into a bowl and beat together until light and fluffy. Gradually beat in the egg yolks and stir in the prepared nuts. Dissolve the coffee in the warm milk then stir it into the mixture. Carefully fold in the flour.

Step four In a separate clean bowl, whisk the egg whites until they form soft peaks and then gently fold into the mixture. Turn the cake mixture into the prepared tin.

Step five Bake for about 25 minutes or until well risen and the top of the cake springs back when lightly pressed with a finger. Leave to cool in the tin for a few minutes then turn out, peel off the parchment and finish cooling on a wire rack.

Step six Meanwhile, prepare the filling. Peel, core and slice the apples and put them in a pan with the apricot jam, lemon zest and juice. Cover and cook very gently until the apples are soft but still retain their shape. Leave to cool.

Step seven Cut the cake in half horizontally and sandwich the slices together with the cooled apple mixture. Melt the chocolate gently in a bowl set over a pan of hot water, stirring occasionally. Spread over the top of the cake and leave to set. Serve with cream or crème fraîche.

Wimbledon Cake

This cake is perfect not just for the Wimbledon tennis season, but for all summer occasions too. It uses no flour, and the semolina used instead gives it a slightly crunchy, close texture. The cake must be eaten on the day of filling.

Step one Preheat the oven to 180°C/Fan 160°C/gas 4. Grease the tin then line the base with non-stick baking parchment.

Step two Measure the egg yolks, sugar, orange zest and juice and the semolina into a bowl and beat until thoroughly blended. In a separate clean bowl, whisk the egg whites until they are stiff but not dry, then gently fold into the orange and semolina mixture. Turn into the prepared tin.

Step three Bake for 30–35 minutes or until well risen and the top of the cake springs back when lightly pressed with a finger. Leave to cool in the tin for a few minutes then turn out, peel off the parchment and finish cooling on a wire rack.

Step four Reserve a few strawberries to decorate the top of the cake, then slice the remainder. Halve the passion fruit and scoop out the pulp. To fill the cold cake, cut it in half horizontally and sandwich the slices together with the sliced strawberries, passion fruit pulp and whipped cream. Just before serving, decorate with the reserved strawberries, sliced or left whole, and sift some icing sugar over the top.

Cake tin needed:
a deep, round 20cm (8in) cake tin

3 large eggs, separated

100g (4oz) caster sugar

zest and juice of 1 orange

75g (3oz) semolina

for the filling and topping

100g (4oz) strawberries

1 passion fruit

150ml (¼ pint) whipping or pouring double cream, whipped

icing sugar, for dusting

Have you made this recipe? Tell us what you think at
www.mykitchentable.co.uk/blog

KITCHEN
TABLE

171

Gâteau Moka aux Amandes

This is one of my favourite coffee cakes, and it looks spectacular, too. Add a little brandy to the filling, if you like.

Cake tin needed:
a deep, round 23cm (9in) cake tin

3 large eggs

100g (4oz) caster sugar

75g (3oz) self-raising flour

for the crème au beurre moka

75g (3oz) caster sugar

4 tbsp water

2 large egg yolks

175g (6oz) butter, softened

1–2 tbsp coffee essence

to finish

175g (6oz) shredded or flaked toasted almonds

icing sugar, for dusting (optional)

Step one Preheat the oven to 190°C/Fan 170°C/gas 5. Grease the tin then line the base with non-stick baking parchment.

Step two Measure the eggs and sugar into a large bowl and whisk at full speed until the mixture is pale in colour and thick enough to just leave a trail when the whisk is lifted. Sift the flour over the surface of the mixture and gently fold in with a metal spoon or spatula. Turn into the prepared tin.

Step three Bake for about 30 minutes or until well risen and the top of the cake springs back when lightly pressed with a finger. Leave to cool in the tin for a few minutes then turn out, peel off the parchment and finish cooling on a wire rack.

Step four To make the crème au beurre moka (coffee butter cream), measure the sugar and water into a small heavy-based pan. Heat very gently until the sugar has dissolved. Bring to the boil then boil steadily for 2–3 minutes until it has reached a temperature of 107°C on a sugar thermometer, or until the syrup forms a slim thread when pulled apart between two teaspoons.

Step five Place the egg yolks into a bowl and give them a quick stir to break them up. Pour the syrup in a thin stream onto the egg yolks, whisking all the time. Continue to whisk until the mixture is thick and cold. In another bowl, cream the butter until very soft and gradually beat in the egg yolk mixture. Stir in the coffee essence to flavour.

Step six Cut the cold cake in half horizontally and sandwich the slices together with a thin layer of the coffee butter cream. Spread butter cream over the top and sides of the cake as well, retaining some for decoration, then press the toasted almonds all over the cake. Dust lightly with icing sugar, if you like, and pipe rosettes of the remaining butter cream around the top.

Raspberry Meringue Roulade

This is rather an unusual idea, and it makes a generous roulade, an excellent size for a party. It also freezes extremely well. Simply wrap in foil to freeze, then allow about 8 hours to thaw before serving.

Step one Preheat the oven to 220°C/Fan 200°C/gas 7. Line the tin with non-stick baking parchment.

Step two Whisk the egg whites until very stiff. Gradually add the sugar, a teaspoon at a time, whisking well between each addition. Whisk until very, very stiff and all the sugar has been added.

Step three Spread the meringue mixture into the prepared tin and sprinkle with the almonds. Place the tin fairly near the top of the preheated oven and bake for about 8 minutes until pale golden. Then reduce the oven temperature to 160°C/325°F/gas 3 and bake the roulade for a further 15 minutes until firm to the touch.

Step four Remove the meringue from the oven and turn it almond side down onto a sheet of non-stick baking parchment. Remove the parchment from the base of the cooked meringue and allow to cool for about 10 minutes.

Step five While the meringue is cooling, whisk the cream until it stands in stiff peaks, and gently mix in the raspberries. Spread the cream and raspberries evenly over the cooled meringue. Start to roll from the long end fairly tightly until rolled up like a roulade. Wrap in non-stick baking parchment and chill before serving.

Leftover egg yolks should be stored in the fridge in a small container. Pour a tablespoon of cold water over the top, and then cover with clingfilm. Use within a week.

Cake tin needed:
a 33 x 23cm (13 x 9in)
Swiss roll tin

5 large egg whites

275g (10oz) caster
sugar

50g (2oz) flaked
almonds

for the filling
300ml (½ pint)
whipping or pouring
double cream

350g (12oz) fresh
raspberries

For more recipes from My Kitchen Table, sign up for our newsletter at www.mykitchentable.co.uk/newsletter

American Chocolate Ripple Cheesecake

This cheesecake is quite sweet and rich and so should be served in small portions. Expect the cheesecake to crack on cooling.

Cake tin needed:
a 20cm (8in) loose-based cake tin or springform tin

for the base

100g (4oz) plain chocolate digestive biscuits

50g (2oz) butter

for the cheesecake

150g (5oz) plain chocolate (39 per cent cocoa solids)

675g (1½lb) full-fat soft cheese

225g (8oz) caster sugar

½ tsp vanilla extract

2 large eggs

Step one Preheat the oven to 160°C/Fan 140°C/gas 3. Lightly grease the tin.

Step two Put the biscuits into a plastic bag and crush finely with a rolling pin. Melt the butter in a medium-sized pan. Remove the pan from the heat and stir in the biscuit crumbs. Press into the prepared tin and leave to set.

Step three To make the cheesecake filling, break the chocolate into pieces and melt gently in a bowl set over a pan of hot water, stirring occasionally. Cool slightly. Measure the cheese into a large bowl and beat until soft. Add the sugar and beat again until well mixed. Beat in the vanilla extract and then the eggs, one at a time.

Step four Spoon half the cheese mixture onto the biscuit crust in dollops, separating the spoonfuls. Add the melted chocolate to the remaining cheese mixture and stir well to mix. Spoon this chocolate mixture in between the plain mixture. Swirl the top with a knife to give a marbled effect.

Step five Bake for about 30 minutes or until the cheesecake becomes puffy around the edges but is still very soft in the centre. Turn off the oven but leave the cheesecake in the oven to cool. Chill well and then loosen the cheesecake from the sides of the tin using a small palette knife. Serve well chilled.

Chocolate, Brandy and Ginger Cheesecake

A sophisticated cheesecake. If you like, you can add a little more brandy to the cheesecake filling.

Step one Lightly grease the tin.

Step two Put the biscuits into a plastic bag and crush finely with a rolling pin. Melt the butter in a medium-sized pan. Remove the pan from the heat and stir in the biscuit crumbs and sugar. Press into the prepared tin and leave to set.

Step three To make the cheesecake filling, melt the chocolate gently in a bowl set over a pan of hot water, stirring occasionally. Allow to cool slightly.

Step four Sprinkle the gelatine over the measured water in a small bowl and leave for 10 minutes to 'sponge'. Stand the bowl in a pan of gently simmering water until the gelatine has completely dissolved. Leave to cool slightly.

Step five Beat together the egg yolks, sugar and cheese in a large bowl. Add the soured cream and cooled chocolate. Stir in the dissolved gelatine. Whisk the egg whites until frothy and fold into the cheese mixture along with the brandy and chopped fresh ginger. Pour onto the biscuit base and chill in the fridge to set.

Step six When set, carefully remove the cheesecake from the tin before decorating with whipped cream, chocolate curls and slices of stem ginger.

Cake tin needed: a 20cm (8in) loose-based cake tin or springform tin

for the base

100g (4oz) ginger biscuits

50g (2oz) butter

25g (1oz) demerara sugar

for the cheesecake

100g (4oz) plain chocolate (39 per cent cocoa solids)

15g (½ oz) sachet powdered gelatine

3 tbsp cold water

2 large eggs, separated

50g (2oz) caster sugar

100g (4oz) full-fat soft cheese

150ml (¼ pint) soured cream

4 tbsp brandy

about 25g (1oz) fresh ginger, finely chopped

to decorate

150ml (¼ pint) pouring double cream, whipped

chocolate curls (see page 52)

a few slices of stem ginger

Buttermilk and Honey Cheesecake

This is a lovely, subtly flavoured cooked cheesecake. You'll find buttermilk in supermarkets, with the yoghurts and creams.

Cake tin needed:
a 20cm (8in) loose-based cake tin or springform tin

for the base
1 sponge flan case, about 20cm (8in) in diameter

for the cheesecake
225g (8oz) full-fat soft cheese

3 large eggs, separated

75g (3oz) caster sugar

2 rounded tbsp clear honey, plus 1 tbsp honey, to glaze

50g (2oz) ground almonds

40g (1½ oz) plain flour

300ml (½ pint) buttermilk

a handful of flaked almonds

Step one Preheat the oven to 160°C/Fan 140°C/gas 3. Lightly grease the tin. Slip the sponge flan case into the prepared tin, trimming the cake to fit if necessary.

Step two Measure the cheese into a large bowl and beat until soft. Beat in the egg yolks along with 25g (1oz) of the sugar, the honey, ground almonds, flour and buttermilk. In a separate bowl, whisk the egg whites until stiff, then whisk in the remaining sugar. Fold into the cheese mixture. Spoon the mixture onto the sponge flan case and sprinkle the flaked almonds over the surface.

Step three Bake for about 1¼ hours or until firm but still spongy to the touch. Turn off the oven, open the door and leave the cheesecake to cool inside.

Step four When the cheesecake is cool, take it out of the oven, ease it away from the sides of the tin with a small palette knife and slide onto a serving plate. Gently heat the extra tablespoon of honey in a small pan and brush over the top of the cheesecake to glaze.

Hazelnut Meringue Cake

This has become a classic favourite, the raspberries and hazelnuts being a particularly good combination. Fill the meringue about 3 hours before serving; it will then cut into portions without splintering.

Step one Preheat the oven to 190°C/Fan 170°C/gas 5. Lightly grease the tins and then line the bases with non-stick baking parchment.

Step two Place the hazelnuts on a baking sheet and put in the oven for about 10 minutes, then tip onto a clean tea towel and rub well together to remove the skins. (Some stubborn ones may need to go back into the oven but don't worry about getting every last bit of skin off, it's not necessary.) Grind the nuts in a food processor.

Step three Whisk the egg whites until stiff. Add the sugar, a teaspoonful at a time, whisking well between each addition. Whisk until the mixture is very stiff, stands in peaks, and all the sugar has been added. Whisk in the vanilla extract and wine vinegar then fold in the prepared nuts. Divide the mixture between the tins and level the surface with a palette knife.

Step four Bake for 30–40 minutes, but no longer. The top of the meringue will be crisp and the inside soft and marshmallow-like. Turn out of the tins and leave to cool on a wire rack.

Step five To make the filling, whisk the cream until thick. Use about two-thirds to sandwich the meringues together, along with two-thirds of the raspberries. Spread the remaining cream over the top, scatter on the remaining raspberries and dust with icing sugar. Serve with raspberry coulis, if you like.

If you don't have sandwich tins, you can cook the mixture on two flat baking sheets, spread out into two circles. It won't look quite so neat, but it tastes the same! Walnuts can be used in place of the hazelnuts in the meringue. Choose a fruit to complement the walnuts, such as strawberries or ripe peaches in season.

Cake tins needed:
2 x 20cm (8in) sandwich tins

140g (4½ oz) shelled hazelnuts

4 large egg whites

250g (9oz) caster sugar

a few drops of vanilla extract

½ tsp white wine vinegar

for the filling

300ml (½ pint) whipping or pouring double cream, whipped

225g (8oz) fresh **raspberries**

icing sugar, for dusting

Raspberry coulis, to serve (optional)

American Cheesecake

This is a very quick and easy cheesecake to make. It's delicious to eat, too, as the yoghurt gives the filling a wonderfully fresh flavour.

Cake tin needed:
a 20cm (8in) loose-based cake tin or springform tin

for the base

175g (6oz) digestive biscuits

75g (3oz) butter

40g (1½ oz) demerara sugar

for the cheesecake

225g (8oz) full-fat soft cheese

25g (1oz) caster sugar

150ml (¼ pint) pouring double cream

150ml (¼ pint) Greek yoghurt

juice of 1½ lemons

for the topping

175g (6oz) fresh raspberries or other soft fruits

about 4 tbsp redcurrant jelly

Step one Put the biscuits into a plastic bag and crush finely with a rolling pin. Melt the butter in a medium-sized pan. Remove the pan from the heat and stir in the biscuit crumbs and sugar. Press over the base and sides of the tin, then leave to set.

Step two To make the cheesecake filling, measure the cheese and sugar into a large bowl (or food processor) and mix well to blend thoroughly. Add the cream and yoghurt and mix again. Gradually add the lemon juice, whisking all the time. Turn the mixture into the tin over the biscuit crust, level the surface, and chill in the fridge overnight to set.

Step three Run a knife round the edge of the biscuit crust to loosen the cheesecake, then push up the base or remove the sides of the tin and slide the cheesecake onto a serving plate.

Step four Arrange the fruit on top of the cheesecake. Heat the redcurrant jelly in a small saucepan until it has melted, and then carefully brush over the fruit. Leave to set. Serve chilled.

Austrian Curd Cheesecake

This makes a good deep cheesecake. It is very moist, so there is no need for cream.

Step one Preheat the oven to 190°C/Fan 170°C/gas 5. Lightly grease the tin and then line the base with non-stick baking parchment.

Step two Soften the butter well in a large bowl and then add the sugar and curd cheese or ricotta. Beat well together until light and creamy. Beat the egg yolks into the mixture one at a time, then stir in the ground almonds, sultanas, semolina and the grated lemon zest and juice.

Step three Leave the mixture to stand for about 10 minutes. (This allows the mixture to thicken so that the sultanas don't sink to the base of the cake during baking.)

Step four In a separate bowl, whisk the egg whites until stiff but not dry and fold lightly into the mixture. Turn the mixture into the prepared tin.

Step five Bake for about 1 hour or until firm to the touch. Cover the top of the cheesecake loosely with foil about halfway through the cooking time to prevent the top from becoming too brown.

Step six When the cheesecake is cooked, turn off the oven but leave the cheesecake inside to cool for about 1 hour. Allow to cool completely, then loosen the sides of the cake with a palette knife and remove the sides of the tin. Invert the cheesecake, remove the base of the tin, peel off the parchment and turn it back the right way up. Dust with sifted icing sugar before serving.

Cake tin needed:
a 23cm (9in) loose-based cake tin or springform tin

150g (5oz) butter, softened

275g (10oz) caster sugar

550g (1¼ lb) curd cheese or ricotta

4 large eggs, separated

100g (4oz) ground almonds

100g (4oz) sultanas

50g (2oz) semolina

zest and juice of 2 lemons

icing sugar, for dusting

Victorian Christmas Cake

Unlike with traditional Christmas cakes, this mixture produces a light, yet succulent cake.

Cake tin needed:
a deep, round 23cm (9in) cake tin

350g (12oz) red or natural glacé cherries

225g (8oz) tin pineapple in natural juice

350g (12oz) ready-to-eat dried apricots

100g (4oz) blanched almonds

zest of 2 lemons

350g (12oz) sultanas

250g (9oz) self-raising flour

250g (9oz) caster sugar

250g (9oz) butter, softened

75g (3oz) ground almonds

5 large eggs

to decorate

blanched almonds

red or natural glacé cherries

glacé pineapple (available from health-food shops)

100g (4oz) sifted icing sugar

Step one Preheat the oven to 160°C/Fan 140°C/gas 3. Grease the tin then line the base and sides with a double layer of non-stick baking parchment.

Step two Cut the cherries into quarters, put in a sieve and rinse under running water then drain well. Drain and roughly chop the pineapple, then dry the pineapple and cherries thoroughly with kitchen paper. Snip the apricots into pieces. Roughly chop the almonds. Place the prepared fruit and nuts in a bowl with the lemon zest and sultanas and gently mix together.

Step three Measure the remaining ingredients into a large bowl and beat well for 1 minute until smooth. Lightly fold in the fruit and nuts then turn the mixture into the prepared cake tin. Level the surface and decorate the top with blanched whole almonds, halved glacé cherries and pieces of glacé pineapple.

Step four Bake for about 2¼ hours or until golden brown. A skewer inserted into the centre of the cake should come out clean. Cover the cake loosely with foil after 1 hour to prevent the top becoming too dark. Leave to cool in the tin for 30 minutes then turn out, peel off the parchment and finish cooling on a wire rack. Mix the icing sugar with a little water, and drizzle over the cake to glaze.

KITCHEN TABLE

Have you made this recipe? Tell us what you think at www.mykitchentable.co.uk/blog

Fast Mincemeat Christmas Cake

I've often been asked for this recipe, which doesn't have to be made in advance or fed with brandy. The cake is light and moist. Cover it with marzipan and fondant icing, and finish with a ribbon and bow. This cake needs 900g (2lb) marzipan and fondant icing to cover.

Step one Preheat the oven to 160°C/Fan 140°C/gas 3. Lightly grease the tin then line the base and sides with non-stick baking parchment.

Step two Measure all the cake ingredients into a large bowl and beat well for 1 minute until thoroughly mixed. Turn into the prepared tin and level the surface.

Step three Bake for about 1¾ hours or until a skewer inserted into the centre comes out clean and the cake is shrinking from the sides of the tin. Cover the cake with foil after 1 hour if it's beginning to brown too much. Leave to cool in the tin for 10 minutes then turn out, peel off the parchment and finish cooling on a wire rack.

Step four Cover the cake with almond paste or marzipan about a week before icing. Cover with fondant icing then decorate the cake with ribbon.

There are some excellent makes of fondant or ready-made icing available. However, if you prefer to make your own here is a recipe that makes 550g (1¼lb) of fondant icing: sift 500g (1lb 2oz) icing sugar into a large mixing bowl. Make a well in the centre and add 1 generous tablespoon of liquid glucose and 1 large egg white. Knead together until the mixture forms a soft ball. Turn out onto a work surface lightly dusted with icing sugar and knead for about 10 minutes until smooth and brilliant white. Wrap in clingfilm and store in the fridge until required.

Cookware needed:
a 25cm (10in) round silver cake board

Cake tin needed:
a deep, round 20cm (8in) cake tin

150g (5oz) butter, softened

150g (5oz) light muscovado sugar

2 large eggs

225g (8oz) self-raising flour

400g (14oz) luxury mincemeat

175g (6oz) currants

50g (3oz) chopped almonds

to decorate

900g (2lb) almond paste or marzipan (see page 199)

900g (2 lb) fondant icing

ribbon, to decorate

Bûche de Noël

This is a version of the French Christmas log, which is suitable for serving as a dessert or with coffee.

Cake tin needed:
a baking sheet

1 unfilled Chocolate Swiss Roll (see page 8)

for the filling

1 tbsp coffee essence

4 tbsp hot milk

225g (8oz) unsweetened chestnut purée

50g (2oz) caster sugar

150ml (¼ pint) whipping or pouring double cream, whipped

2 tbsp brandy

for the topping

300ml (½ pint) whipping or pouring double cream, whipped

cocoa powder, to dust

holly leaves, to decorate

Step one First make the Chocolate Swiss Roll (page 8). Roll with non-stick baking parchment inside and leave to cool.

Step two While the cake is cooling, make the filling. Mix the coffee essence with the milk. Push the chestnut purée through a seive into a bowl and beat in the coffee mixture and the sugar until the mixture is smooth. Fold the whipped cream into the chestnut purée along with the brandy.

Step three Carefully unroll the Swiss roll, remove the parchment and spread the chestnut filling all over the cake, then re-roll. Cut a small slice off at an angle from one of the ends of the Swiss roll, place the Swiss roll onto a serving plate or board, and attach the slice to look like a branch.

Step four Spread the whipped cream over the cake to cover completely, using a small palette knife in long strokes to give the bark effect. Dust lightly with cocoa and decorate with holly leaves.

Tiny Fruit Cakes

Individual fruit cakes make delightful Christmas gifts.

Step one Cut the cherries into quarters, put in a sieve and rinse under running water. Drain well then dry thoroughly with kitchen paper. Measure all the dried fruits into a large bowl, add the brandy, rum or sherry, cover the bowl tightly and leave overnight.

Step two Preheat the oven to 160°C/Fan 140°C/gas 3. Grease the tins then line the bases and sides with non-stick baking parchment.

Step three Measure the chopped and ground almonds, lemon zest, flour, mixed spice, sugar, butter, treacle and egg into large bowl and mix together. Beat thoroughly for about 2 minutes until the mixture is smooth. Add the soaked fruit and any remaining liquid to the bowl and stir to mix in thoroughly. Spoon the mixture into the prepared tins, spreading it evenly. Level the surfaces and then sprinkle with flaked almonds.

Step four Bake for 1–1¼ hours or until a fine skewer inserted into the centre comes out clean. Allow the cakes to cool in the tins. Pierce the top of the cakes in several places with a skewer and spoon in a little brandy, rum or sherry.

Step five Remove the cakes from the tins but do not remove the non-stick baking parchment as this helps to keep the cakes moist. Wrap in more non-stick baking parchment and then some foil, and store in a cool place for a week.

Step six Push the apricot jam through a sieve into a small pan and warm it slightly, then brush it over the surface of the cakes. Cover with almond paste and icing, as on page 200. Decorate as liked.

Makes 3 cakes

Cake tins needed:
3 x 220g tins (baked bean tins are ideal), washed and dried, labels removed

40g (1½ oz) red or natural glacé cherries

50g (2oz) raisins

50g (2oz) sultanas

50g (2oz) currants

25g (1oz) ready-to-eat dried apricots

15g (½ oz) chopped candied peel

2 tsp brandy, rum or sherry, plus extra for feeding the cakes

15g (½ oz) chopped almonds

15g (½ oz) ground almonds

zest of ¼ lemon

75g (3oz) plain flour

½ level tsp ground mixed spice

50g (2oz) dark muscovado sugar

50g (2oz) butter, softened

2 tsp black treacle

1 large egg

1 tbsp flaked almonds

for the icing

3 tbsp apricot jam

225g (8oz) almond paste (see page 199)

225g (8oz) fondant icing (see page 191)

Jane's Fruit Cake

This is a good family cake. It goes quite dark when baked because of the wholemeal flour.

Cake tin needed:
a deep, round 23cm
(9in) cake tin

200g (7oz) butter,
softened

350g (12oz) light
muscovado sugar

3 large eggs

450g (1lb) self-raising
wholemeal flour

150ml (¼ pint)
buttermilk

350g (12oz) sultanas

350g (12oz) currants

50g (2oz) flaked
almonds, for
sprinkling

Step one Preheat the oven to 140°C/Fan 120°C/gas 1. Grease the tin and line the base and sides with a double layer of non-stick baking parchment.

Step two Measure all the cake ingredients, except the flaked almonds, into a large bowl and mix thoroughly. Beat the mixture for 2–3 minutes until smooth and glossy. Spoon into the prepared tin and level the surface. Sprinkle with the flaked almonds.

Step three Bake for 3–3½ hours or until a skewer inserted into the centre comes out clean. Leave to cool in the tin then turn out, but leave the parchment on as this helps to keep the cake moist.

Step four To store, wrap the cake in more non-stick baking parchment and then some foil, and keep in a cool place.

Have you made this recipe? Tell us what you think at
www.mykitchentable.co.uk/blog

KITCHEN
TABLE

196

Easter Simnel Cake

This has become the traditional Easter cake, but originally it was given by servant girls to their mothers when they went home on Mothering Sunday. The almond-paste balls represent the eleven apostles (not including Judas).

Step one Preheat the oven to 150°C/Fan 130°C/gas 2. Lightly grease the tin then line the base and sides with non-stick baking parchment.

Step two Cut the cherries into quarters, put in a sieve and rinse under running water. Drain well then dry thoroughly with kitchen paper. Measure all the cake ingredients into a large mixing bowl and beat well until thoroughly blended. Place half the mixture into the prepared tin and level the surface.

Step three Take one-third of the almond paste and roll it out to a circle the size of the tin and then place on top of the cake mixture. Spoon the remaining cake mixture on top and level the surface.

Step four Bake for about 2½ hours until well risen, evenly brown and firm to the touch. Cover with foil after 1 hour if the top is browning too quickly. Leave to cool in the tin for 10 minutes then turn out, peel off the parchment and finish cooling on a wire rack.

Step five When the cake is cool, brush the top with a little warmed apricot jam and roll out half the remaining almond paste to fit the top. Press firmly on the top and crimp the edges to decorate. Mark a criss-cross pattern on the almond paste with a sharp knife. Form the remaining almond paste into 11 balls. Brush the almond paste with beaten egg and arrange the almond paste balls around the edge of the cake. Brush the tops of the balls with beaten egg, too, and then place the cake under a hot grill to turn the almond paste golden.

You can now buy good ready-made almond paste and marzipan, but if you want to make your own try this simple recipe, which makes 675g (1½lb) almond paste: mix 225g (8oz) ground almonds with 4 large egg yolks (or 2 whole large eggs) and 6 drops of almond extract. Knead to form a stiff paste, wrap in clingfilm and store in the fridge until required.

Cake tin needed:
a deep, round 20cm (8in) cake tin

100g (4oz) red or natural glacé cherries

225g (8oz) butter, softened

225g (8oz) light muscovado sugar

4 large eggs

225g (8oz) self-raising flour

225g (8oz) sultanas

100g (4oz) currants

50g (2oz) chopped candied peel

zest of 2 lemons

2 level tsp ground mixed spice

for the filling and topping

450g (1lb) almond paste or marzipan

2 tbsp apricot jam

1 large egg, beaten, to glaze

Sponge Christening Cake

A lemon cake is perfect for a christening. Colour the icing pale pink or pale blue, if you like, or maybe a pale primrose yellow.

Cake tin needed:
a deep, round 23cm (9in) cake tin

75g (3oz) butter

6 large eggs

175g (6oz) caster sugar

150g (5oz) self-raising flour

2 level tbsp cornflour

for the filling

300ml (½ pint) whipping or pouring double cream, whipped

4 tbsp lemon curd

to finish

900g (2lb) fondant icing (see page 191)

crystallized flowers and ribbon, to decorate

Step one Preheat the oven to 180°C/Fan 160°C/gas 4. Grease the tin then line the base with non-stick baking parchment.

Step two Melt the butter in a small pan and then leave it to cool slightly. Measure the eggs and sugar into a large bowl and whisk over hot water until the mixture becomes pale and creamy and thick enough to leave a trail on the surface when the whisk is lifted. Remove the bowl from the pan and continue to whisk until the mixture is cold.

Step three Sift the flours together into a bowl. Fold half the flour into the egg mixture with a metal spoon, then carefully pour half the cooled butter around the edge of the mixture and lightly fold in. Fold in the remaining flour and butter in the same manner. Pour into the prepared tin and level the surface.

Step four Bake for about 40 minutes or until well risen, firm to the touch and beginning to shrink away from the sides of the tin. Leave to cool in the tin for a few minutes then turn out, peel off the parchment and finish cooling on a wire rack.

Step five With a long sharp knife, cut the cake into three horizontally. To make the filling, reserve 3–4 tablespoons of the whipped cream then mix the remainder with the lemon curd and use to sandwich the cake slices. Put the cake on a serving plate or board. Spread the reserved cream around the sides and over the top of the cake, just enough to make the surfaces sticky.

Step six Dust the work surface with icing sugar and roll out the icing large enough to cover the cake completely. Fold the icing over the rolling pin and carefully lift onto the cake, gently smoothing the sides. Trim the extra icing from the base of the cake. Decorate with ribbon and crystallized flowers.

Celebration Cake

I use this recipe for Christmas, birthdays and all special occasions – it's a winner.

Step one Put the currants, sultanas, raisins, cherries, apricots and mixed peel into a large bowl. Stir in the brandy, cover the bowl and leave in a cool place overnight.

Step two Preheat the oven to 140°C/Fan 120°C/gas 1. Lightly grease the cake tin. Cut a strip of non-stick baking parchment to fit twice around the sides of the tin. Fold the base edge of the strip up by about 2.5cm (1in), creasing it firmly, then open out the fold and cut slanting lines into this narrow strip at intervals. Put a circle of non-stick baking parchment into the base of the tin, lightly grease the outer edge and then fit the prepared strip of parchment with the snipped edge in the base of the tin to line the sides. Place a second circle of non-stick baking parchment in the tin to cover the cut part of the paper.

Step three Measure all the remaining cake ingredients into a large bowl and beat well to mix thoroughly; an electric mixer is best for this, but of course you can also beat by hand with a wooden spoon. Fold in the soaked fruits. Spoon the mixture into the prepared cake tin and spread out evenly with the back of the spoon. Decorate the top with blanched almonds and halved glacé cherries, pushing them lightly into the top of the cake mixture.

Step four Cover the top of the cake loosely with a double layer of non-stick baking parchment and bake for 4–4½ hours, until the cake feels firm to the touch and a skewer inserted into the centre comes out clean. Allow the cake to cool in the tin. When the cake is almost cold, remove it from the tin and peel off the parchment. Pierce the base at intervals with a fine skewer and feed with a little brandy. Once the cake is completely cold, wrap it in a double layer of non-stick baking parchment and then in foil. Store in a cool place for up to 3 months, feeding at intervals with more brandy.

Cake tin needed:
a deep, round 23cm (9in) cake tin

350g (12oz) currants

225g (8oz) each sultanas and raisins

175g (6oz) each glacé cherries, quartered, rinsed and dried and ready-to-eat dried apricots, snipped into pieces

75g (3oz) mixed candied peel, finely chopped

4 tbsp brandy, plus extra to 'feed' the cake

275g (10oz) plain flour

scant ½ level tsp grated nutmeg

¼ level tsp ground mixed spice

400g (14oz) butter, softened

400g (14oz) dark muscovado sugar

5 large eggs

65g (2½ oz) chopped almonds

1 tbsp black treacle

zest of 1 lemon and 1 orange

to decorate

whole blanched almonds

glacé cherries, halved, rinsed and dried

Divine Chocolate Birthday Cake

This is a very close-textured 'fudgy' cake that needs no filling. There is no flour in this recipe; ground almonds give the flavour and texture.

Cake tin needed:
a deep, round 23cm (9in) cake tin

6 large eggs, 5 of them separated

215g (7½ oz) caster sugar

265g (9½ oz) plain chocolate (39 per cent cocoa solids), broken into pieces

1 level tsp instant coffee powder

1 tsp hot water

150g (5oz) ground almonds

for the icing

4 tbsp apricot jam

225g (8oz) plain chocolate (39 per cent cocoa solids), broken into pieces

100g (4oz) unsalted butter

Step one Preheat the oven to 190°C/Fan 170°C/gas 5. Grease the tin then line the base with non-stick baking parchment.

Step two Place the egg yolks and whole egg in a large bowl with the sugar and beat together until thick and light in colour. Melt the chocolate gently in a heatproof bowl set over a pan of simmering water, stirring occasionally. Dissolve the coffee granules in the water and add to the melted chocolate. Cool slightly, then stir into the egg mixture along with the ground almonds.

Step three In a separate bowl, whisk the egg whites until stiff but not dry. Carefully fold into the egg and chocolate mixture. Turn into the prepared tin and gently level the surface.

Step four Bake for about 50 minutes or until well risen, and a skewer inserted into the centre comes out clean. Leave to cool in the tin for 10 minutes then turn out, peel off the parchment and finish cooling on a wire rack.

Step five Measure the apricot jam into a small saucepan and allow to melt over a low heat. Brush over the cake. To make the icing, melt the chocolate gently in a bowl set over a pan of hot water, stirring occasionally. Add the butter and stir until the icing has the consistency of thick pouring cream, cooling if necessary. Stand the wire rack on a baking sheet to catch any drips, then pour the icing over the cake, smoothing it over the top and sides with a palette knife. Allow to set, then decorate if you like.

For a video masterclass on icing a cake, go to www.mykitchentable.co.uk/videos/icing

10 9 8 7

Published in 2011 by BBC Books,
an imprint of Ebury Publishing.
A Random House Group company

Recipes © Mary Berry 2011
Book design © Woodlands Books Ltd 2011

All recipes contained in this book first appeared in *Mary Berry's Quick and Easy Cakes* (1993), *Mary Berry's Ultimate Cake Book* (1994), *Mary Berry Cooks Puddings and Desserts* (1997), *Mary Berry Cooks Cakes* (1998) and *Mary Berry Foolproof Cakes* (2004). Mary Berry has asserted her right to be identified as the author of this Work in accordance with the Copyright, Designs and Patents Act 1988

The Random House Group Limited
Reg. No. 954009

Addresses for companies within the Random House Group can be found at www.randomhouse.co.uk

A CIP catalogue record for this book is available from the British Library

The Random House Group Limited supports the Forest Stewardship Council (FSC®), the leading international forest certification organisation. Our books carrying the FSC label are printed on FSC® certified paper. FSC is the only forest certification scheme endorsed by the leading environmental organisations, including Greenpeace. Our paper procurement policy can be found at ·www.randomhouse.co.uk/environment

To buy books by your favourite authors and register for offers visit www.rbooks.co.uk

Printed and bound in the UK by Butler, Tanner and Dennis Ltd

Colour origination by AltaImage

Commissioning Editor: Muna Reyal

Project Editor: Laura Higginson

Designer: Lucy Stephens

Photographer: William Reavell © Woodlands Books Ltd 2011 (see also credits below)

Food Stylist: Annie Rigg

Props Stylist: Liz Belton

Copy-editor: Michele Clarke

Production: Helen Everson

Photography on page 4 © Muir Vidler; pages 6, 10, 13, 17, 18, 21, 26, 30, 33, 41, 42, 54, 58, 62, 78, 85, 114, 123, 126, 146, 153, 202 © Jean Cazals; 9, 15, 22, 25, 34, 37, 49, 50, 53, 57, 69, 74, 77, 81, 82, 130, 149, 165, 170, 178, 182, 186, 189, 197, 198, 201 © Dan Jones; 29, 86, 89 © James Murphy; 4 by Muir Vidler, 174 by Philip Webb and 93, 97, 117, 161, 162 by Juliet Piddington © Woodlands Books Ltd.

ISBN: 978 1 849 90149 9